Beginning
Deno
Development

Greg Lim

Table of Contents

PREFACE

About this book

In this book, we take you on a fun, hands-on and pragmatic journey to learning Deno development. You'll start building your first Deno app within minutes. Every chapter is written in a bite-sized manner and straight to the point as I don't want to waste your time (and most certainly mine) on the content you don't need. In the end, you will have the skills to create a Deno web app and a Deno REST API.

In the course of this book, we will cover:
- Chapter 1: Introduction
- Chapter 2: Introduction to Oak
- Chapter 3: Introducing Templating Engines
- Chapter 4: Styling a User Interface
- Chapter 5: Re-structuring Our App
- Chapter 6: Implementing C.R.U.D. Operations
- Chapter 7: Using MongoDB as Our Database
- Chapter 8: Building Rest APIs with Deno
- Chapter 9: Comparing Deno and Node

The goal of this book is to teach you Deno development in a manageable way without overwhelming you. We focus only on the essentials and cover the material in a hands-on practice manner for you to code along.

Working Through This Book

This book is purposely broken down into nine short chapters where the development process of each chapter will center on different essential topics. The book takes a practical hands-on approach to learning through practice. You learn best when you code along with the examples in the book. Along the way, if you encounter any problems, do drop me a mail at support@i-ducate.com where I will try to answer your query.

Requirements

No previous knowledge of Deno or Node development required, but you should have basic programming knowledge.

Getting Book Updates

To receive updated versions of the book, subscribe to our mailing list by sending a mail to support@i-ducate.com. I try to update my books to use the latest version of software, libraries and update the codes/content in this book. So, do subscribe to my list to receive updated copies!

Code Examples

Where necessary, the relevant source code links are posted at the end of each chapter.

CHAPTER 1: INTRODUCTION

In this book, we will learn about Deno together with Oak and MongoDB and build a Todo app from scratch with them. In the process, we will learn Deno's features, how to build our first basic server, then build a more advanced server to return server-side rendered views with Oak, templating engines and MongoDB. We will also learn how to build a REST API. Through it, you will progress from a beginner to where you can build apps effectively using these technologies.

The App We Will Be Building

We will build a Todo app which lets users create, read, update and delete todo entries (fig. 1):

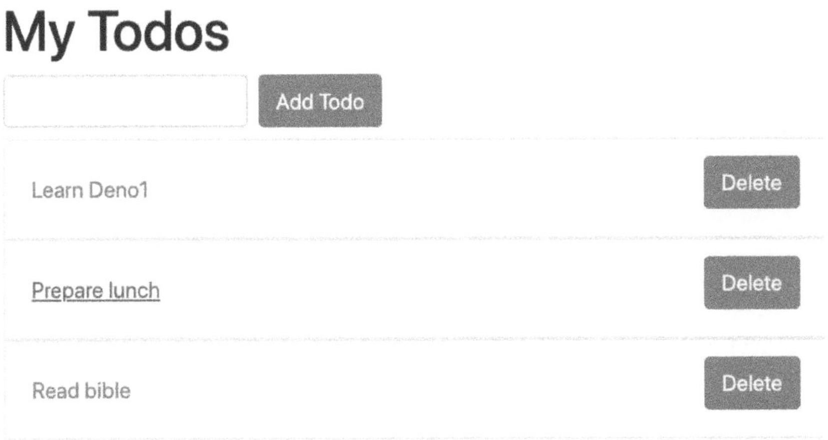

My Todos

	Add Todo
Learn Deno1	Delete
Prepare lunch	Delete
Read bible	Delete

Figure 1

Updating a Todo (fig. 2):

Prepare lunch

Prepare lunch	Update Todo

Figure 2

We will also build a REST API with endpoints to create, read, update and delete products that clients like mobile apps and front-end apps (React, Angular, Vue) can consume.
E.g. *mydomain:8000/products* returns

```
{"products":
  [
  {"id":"5f1d30ca0047230400813ae0",
   "name":"Product 1",
   "description":"Desc 1",
   "price":1.99
  },
  {"id":"5f1fa0a1005572f50082f9b0",
    "name":"Product 2",
    "description":"Desc 2",
    "price":10.99
  },
  {"id":"5f1fa0a800b07a580082f9b1",
    "name":"Product 3",
    "description":"Desc 3",
    "price":5.99
  }
  ]
}
```

Through implementing the web app and REST APIs, we will learn many concepts and solidify our Deno, Oak and MongoDB knowledge.

What is Deno?

Before we understand what Deno is, we need to know how the Internet works. When a user opens up her browser and makes a request to a site, she is known as a client. The client makes a request of a certain website to a server which upon receiving the request, responds with the content of the requested site to the client who then displays it in her browser. For example, I make a request to amazon.com and Amazon servers respond back with the HTML for amazon.com.

There have been server-side programming languages like PHP, Ruby, Python, ASP, Java and others which helps us respond to browser requests appropriately on the server. Traditionally, JavaScript is used to run only on the browser to provide website interactivity for example, dropdown menus. But in

2009, Node.js took V8, Google Chrome's powerful JavaScript engine, out of the browser and enabled it to run on servers. Thus, in addition to the existing server-side languages, developers could now choose JavaScript to develop server-side applications.

Deno like Node is a JavaScript runtime that allows you to run JavaScript code outside of the browser (If you are reading this book, there is a high chance that you have worked with Node before. And even if you have not, don't worry as we will start from scratch). Like Node, Deno is based on Chrome's V8 JavaScript engine, but enriched with server features that let us do things we can't do in the browser. For e.g. interact with files on our local file system.

If you have not already realized, Node and Deno are anagrams of one another. And this is deliberate because Deno was actually created by the creator of Node, and Deno is a deliberate reference to Node. The creator of Node created Deno to fix some of Node's 'flaws'. But it doesn't mean that we got horrible problems in Node and we should all just use Deno. We will revisit this later.

Features of Deno

First, Node by default only supports JavaScript, but Deno on top of JavaScript, also supports TypeScript. The compiler for TypeScript is baked into Deno. So, you can start writing TypeScript and Deno will compile it.

Second, Deno is newer and embraces more modern JavaScript features like TypeScript support, URL imports, promises etc. Because Node is based on older JavaScript code, it doesn't really support promises and typically uses callback functions for asynchronous code. This will be clearer as we progress along this book.

Deno also imposes security permissions on running scripts. By default, a Node script can execute anything, e.g. read/write files without permission. This can be a problem if someone has a malicious intent. Deno is secure by default, meaning that scripts executed by Deno require explicit permission to do certain things for e.g. to read and write files. We explore this in a later section 'Working with Permissions'.

So, should we switch away from Node?

These 'flaws' of Node cannot be so horrible else Node won't be as big and popular as it is. If you do not need the mentioned features, understand that Node is established, has a highly active ecosystem, is used by thousands of companies, has a vast base of maintainers, has a lot of third-party libraries, and is production-proven. It is a fast and secure technology you can use for big apps.

But Deno is here to provide a better version of Node with extra features and solve some of its problems. At the moment, Deno is still pretty new, has a small ecosystem, has a smaller base of maintainers and is not used in production by major companies. But that's doesn't mean that using Deno is a bad choice. In the coming future, we could have a nice co-existence of Deno and Node. So, it brings tremendous opportunities to be an early adopter of Deno.

Easy to Switch to the Other

Deno share many more similarities with Node then differences. And because of the similarities, if you know Deno, it will be quite easy to pick up Node. Conversely, if you know Node, it won't be too difficult to pick up Deno. The key is, no matter which you are learning, you will have a good time learning the other. You can quickly transfer Deno knowledge to Node and vice versa.

Because you are still learning Deno, the similarities and differences that we mention here might seem abstract. Thus, in the last chapter of this book, after having gone through implementing a Deno app, and being more familiar on how Deno works, we will revisit a comparison between Deno and Node which will be more meaningful.

Installing Deno

Before we get started with writing our first Deno program, let's first install Deno. If you visit https://deno.land/ (fig. 3), you will find the Deno home page and installation instructions for it.

Deno

A **secure** runtime for **JavaScript** and **TypeScript**.

Figure 3

https://deno.land/#installation holds the installation instructions for different environments (fig. 4).

Installation

Deno ships as a single executable with no dependencies. You can install it using the installers below, or download a release binary from the releases page.

Shell (Mac, Linux):

```
$ curl -fsSL https://deno.land/x/install/install.sh | sh
```

PowerShell (Windows):

```
$ iwr https://deno.land/x/install/install.ps1 -useb | iex
```

Homebrew (Mac):

```
$ brew install deno
```

Chocolatey (Windows):

```
$ choco install deno
```

Scoop (Windows):

```
$ scoop install deno
```

Build and install from source using Cargo

```
$ cargo install deno
```

See deno_install for more installation options.

Figure 4

You can use any of the approaches depending on your operating system. Because I am using a Mac and am using Homebrew, I will copy-paste the link *brew install deno* into my Terminal. When you do so, it will download and install Deno on your machine.

When the installation is done, as the site suggests, try running a simple program in the Terminal like:

deno run https://deno.land/std/examples/welcome.ts

And you should get the below printed in your Terminal:

Welcome to Deno 🦕

(Note: This application just outputs a text on your command line. However, it also shows you how a

Deno application can be executed from a remote source by downloading and compiling it on the fly)

You can also just type *deno* in the Terminal which will start an interactive environment where you can run Deno code. We won't write code like that in our actual programs of course. We will have our codes in files. But this environment is nice for playing around. For example, you can enter code like in figure 5:

```
users-Air:~ user$ deno
Deno 1.1.3
exit using ctrl+d or close()
> 1+1
2
>
```

Figure 5

Creating our First Server

We will create our first server to handle incoming requests and send back responses.

In a code editor of your choice, (I will be using Visual Studio Code in this book), choose a directory location and in it, create a new file called *first-app.ts*. Fill in the below code to create our first server:

```
import { serve } from "https://deno.land/std@0.63.0/http/server.ts";
const s = serve({ port: 8000 });
console.log("http://localhost:8000/");
for await (const req of s) {
  req.respond({ body: "Hello World\n" });
}
```

And then in the Terminal, run:

```
deno run --allow-net first-app.ts
```

Code Explanation

```
import { serve } from "https://deno.land/std@0.63.0/http/server.ts";
```

Deno supports importing modules from a URL. In the above URL, we import *server.ts* from the *http/server* module. You can actually refer to the source file of *server.ts* at the URL to look at its source code. *server.ts* is built using the core APIs of Deno which you can even do on your own (though not now of course, otherwise you won't be reading my book). But others have done it so that we don't have to re-implement it ourselves.

Note that we have specifically imported the 0.63.0 version (latest version at time of book's writing) instead of just an import for the latest version of *server.ts* (https://deno.land/std/http/server.ts) to ensure that the code in this book doesn't break.

server.ts exports a *serve* function which creates a HTTP web server. You can refer to https://doc.deno.land/https/deno.land/std/http/mod.ts#serve for more documentation of the *serve* function.

```
const s = serve({ port: 8000 });
```

We call the *serve* method and specify in its parameter an object { *port: 8000* } with property *port* to configure the port we want our HTTP server to listen to. *serve* returns a *Server* object which we assign to the variable *s*. You can then use *s* as you would any object.

```
for await (const req of s) {
  req.respond({ body: "Hello World\n" });
}
```

We have a *for* loop to loop through all the requests that our server receives. Notice that we have *await* in the *for* loop. This is to ensure that we await for each request to come in, provide a response, and only then move on to the next request. Note that we also use the *await* keyword without having to wrap it into an *async* function because Deno implements top-level await. This is an example of Deno embracing modern JavaScript features.

We respond to incoming requests with **req.respond({ body: "Hello World\n" })**.

With this code, we can run it to have an on-going server that starts taking requests. That is, the server listens on port 8000 for requests.

Running first-app.ts

To execute the file and start running the server, in Terminal, *cd* to the directory the file is located in and run:

```
deno run --allow-net first-app.ts
```

In our case, for any request made to port 8000, we respond with 'Hello World'. Now go to your browser and enter http://localhost:8000/ (fig. 6). *localhost* in this case refers to our computer which is acting as a local server. But suppose the server is hosted on another computer or site, you can imagine that the link would be http://<computer ip>:8000/.

```
Hello World
```

Figure 6

In your browser, you should see the text 'Hello World' displayed in your browser (fig. 6). This is because we have responded to the request with the code `req.respond({ body: "Hello World\n" })`.

If you look at your Terminal running Deno, you can see 'http://localhost:8000/' being logged. This is because we have the code *`console.log("http://localhost:8000/")`*.

We now have a successful request and respond cycle and I hope that this serves as an introduction to understand how a request and respond works between a client and a server.

Working with Permissions

Notice that we have to specify `--allow-net` to run *first-app.ts*. If we just ran:

```
deno run first-app.ts
```

That is, we omit *--allow-net*, we get an error like: "*Uncaught PermissionDenied: network access to "0.0.0.0:8000", run again with the --allow-net flag*".

By default, Deno scripts cannot read, write files, use environment variables or interact with the network without permissions. In contrast, Node scripts can execute the above without asking for permissions. You have to explicitly assign permission to run Deno scripts. For example, to allow interaction with the network, we have to specify *--allow-net*.

Some other common permissions are:

To allow a script to read files, specify *--allow-read*.

To allow a script to write files, specify *--allow-write*.

We will come across other permissions in the course of this book.

More on Request and Response

Our app currently responds with 'Hello World' regardless of the url entered after *localhost:8000*. To have different responses based on different URLs e.g. *localhost:8000/about*, add the following code in **bold**:

```
import { serve } from "https://deno.land/std@0.63.0/http/server.ts";
const s = serve({ port: 8000 });
console.log("http://localhost:8000/");
for await (const req of s) {
  if(req.url === '/about')
    req.respond({ body: "The about page\n" });
  else if(req.url === '/contact')
    req.respond({ body: "The contact page\n" });
  else if(req.url === '/')
    req.respond({ body: "The home page\n" });
  else {
    req.respond({ body: "page not found\n",status:404 });
  }
}
```

To run the newly added code, we have to stop and restart the server by running again *deno run --allow-net first-app.ts*.

Code Explanation

Using an *if-else* statement in the body of the *for* loop, we check for the request url and depending on its path, we respond with different messages. If the url contains '/about', we serve the *about* text. If it contains '/contact', we serve the *contact* text and if it's just '/', we serve the *home* text. If the path does not exist in the *if-else*, we default to the last *else* clause and respond with 'page not found' and specify the *status* property with 404.

```
req.respond({ body: "page not found\n",status:404 });
```

The *status* property sets the status code of the request. Normally, a status code of 200 indicates that the server responded with a successful response. You can see the status code of your request whenever you request a site from the Chrome browser by going to 'Developer Tools under 'View', 'Developer', 'Developer Tools' (fig. 7).

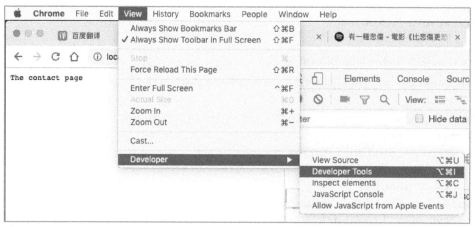

Figure 7

To see your request information, in 'Developer Tools', click on 'Network'. Under 'Status', it will show the status code. In figure 8, I have requested for '/', which is a valid path which returns status code *200* indicatin 'OK'.

Figure 8

If I request for an invalid url like '/contact**s**' (with an extra 's'), it returns the code 404 indicating 'Not Found' (fig. 9).

Figure 9

With this, we can handle different requests from a client and send the appropriate response from the server.

Note that whenever you make changes to file, you need to quit the running server and re-run it because the running server is based on old code. Later on, we will show how to avoid this manual process of quitting and restarting servers.

Responding with HTML

We have been responding to requests with static text. In a real-world setting, we want to respond with HTML. We illustrate how to do so in this section.

Back in *first-app.ts*, add the below code in **bold**:

```
import { serve } from "https://deno.land/std@0.63.0/http/server.ts";
const s = serve({ port: 8000 });
console.log("http://localhost:8000/");
for await (const req of s) {
  const headers = new Headers();
```

```
  headers.set('Content-Type','text/html');
  if(req.url === '/about')
    req.respond({
      body: "<h1>The about page\n</h1>",
      headers: headers
    });
  else if(req.url === '/contact')
    req.respond({
      body: "<h1>The contact page\n</h1>",
      headers: headers
    });
  else if(req.url === '/')
    req.respond({
      body: "<h1>The home page\n</h1>",
      headers: headers
    });
  else {
    req.respond({
      body: "<h1>page not found\n</h1>",
      headers: headers, status:404
    });
  }
}
```

Code Explanation

Instead of *res.respond()* containing a static text, it now contains simple HTML:
`<h1>Home Page</h1>`, `<h1>About Page</h1>`, `<h1>Contact Page</h1>` and `<h1>Page Not Found</h1>`.

```
  headers.set('Content-Type','text/html');
```

We have added headers to our response which contain metadata. The above makes it clear to the browser that we are sending back HTML code. The browser will thus display the HTML correctly and not interpret this as plain text but as HTML.

Running your App

Restart the server with *deno run --allow-net first-app.ts* and we will have HTML presented instead (fig. 10).

The home page

Figure 10

And that is how we respond to requests with HTML.

Is this the way to build large sites?

Notice that we have been using a single script for our entire application:

```
...
for await (const req of s) {
  const headers = new Headers();
  headers.set('Content-Type','text/html');
  if(req.url === '/about')
    req.respond({ body: "<h1>The about page\n</h1>", headers: headers });
  else if(req.url === '/contact')
    req.respond({ body: "<h1>The contact page\n</h1>", headers:
headers });
  else if(req.url === '/')
    req.respond({ body: "<h1>The home page\n</h1>", headers: headers });
  else {
    req.respond({ body: "<h1>page not found\n</h1>", headers: headers,
status:404 });
  }
}
...
```

This script listens to a web browser's requests, either from a computer, mobile phone or any other client consuming our server. We call this script a request handler. When a request comes in, this script looks at the request and decides how to respond.

For small sites, this might seem appropriate, but things quickly get huge and unmanageable as you can imagine, for example, a site like Amazon.com which includes rendering dynamic reusable HTML templates, rendering/uploading of images etc. We explore in the next chapter how Oak helps to solve this problem and make it easier for us to write web applications with Deno.

Deno Visual Studio Code Extension

This section is for those who are using Visual Studio code as their IDE. If you are using another IDE, the steps to install a Deno extension should be similar.

Currently, our Visual Studio Code IDE doesn't recognize Deno. But we can install the Deno extension by going to 'View', 'Extension' and then searching for 'deno' (fig. 11).

Figure 11

After installing the Deno extension, certain errors in your code should be gone. We should also be getting suggestions on what libraries we can use. With the extension, we get a much nicer developer experience with Deno.

Summary

In this chapter, we learned what Deno is and how it's features that make it an improvement over Node. We went through steps to install Deno, created our first server to understand how a request and respond cycle between a client and a server works. We handled requests and responded appropriately with both text and HTML. In the next chapter, we learn about Oak, a middleware framework that makes it easier to develop Deno web applications.

Refer to https://github.com/greglim81/deno_chapter1 for the source code of this chapter. If you face any issues, contact me at support@i-ducate.com.

CHAPTER 2: INTRODUCTION TO OAK

In our app from chapter one, we imported packages (e.g. *http*) from Deno's standard library which is maintained by the Deno team themselves. There are also third-party modules maintained by the community not the (Deno core team) which others can use for their own programs to help work with Deno easier.

These third-party modules are located at the *deno.land* site under the 'Third Party Modules' tab (https://deno.land/x - fig. 1).

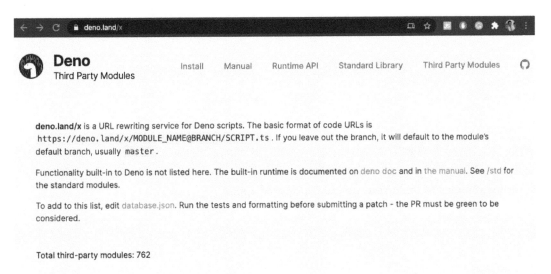

Figure 1

You can search for modules appropriate to use in your code. One essential custom module we will install is Oak. The proper way to build big web apps in Deno is to use Oak and dynamic templates. As you saw in the previous chapter, manually writing HTML directly in our TypeScript code files can be verbose, confusing and limited in features.

Oak is a middleware Deno framework that makes it easier to develop Deno web applications by adding helpful features, organizing our application's functionality with middleware and routing, and facilitates rendering of dynamic HTML views. It is like Express for Node. In the course of the next few chapters, we will explore these features in-depth.

To install Oak, under the 'Third Party Modules' of deno.land, search for 'oak' (fig. 2).

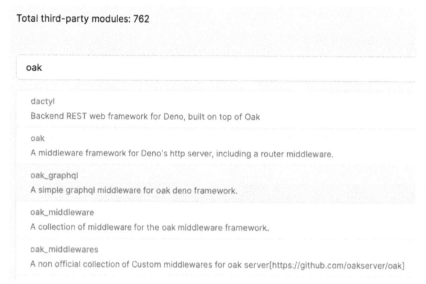

Figure 2

Select 'oak' and there will be instructions on how to install and use it (fig. 3). But I will walk you through the instructions to build your first Oak powered app.

oak

A middleware framework for Deno's http server, including a router middleware.

This middleware framework is inspired by Koa and middleware router inspired by @koa/router.

This README focuses on the mechanics of the oak APIs and is intended for those who are familiar with JavaScript middleware frameworks like Express and Koa as well as a decent understanding of Deno. If you aren't familiar with these, please check out documentation on oakserver.github.io/oak.

Figure 3

Working with Oak

In the project folder from chapter one, create a new file *app.ts* which serves as our root entry file. In it, fill in the below code:

```
import { Application } from "https://deno.land/x/oak/mod.ts";

const app = new Application();

app.use((ctx) => {
  ctx.response.body = "Hello World!";
});

// 'listen' starts the server and starts processing requests
await app.listen({ port: 8000 });
```

The above code serves the same functionality as the code we have earlier implemented (shown below):

```
import { serve } from "https://deno.land/std@0.63.0/http/server.ts";

const s = serve({ port: 8000 });

for await (const req of s) {
  req.respond({ body: "Hello World\n" });
}
```

Now, how is the code using Oak, better than what we have in chapter one? The answer will be better understood as we get through this book. For now, we have a very useful feature using Oak which is middlewares. If you are familiar with Node, you will know about middlewares. But don't fret if you are unfamiliar with it.

A middleware is a function in the middle after the incoming request, which then produces an output that could either be the final output or be used by the next middleware. We can register middlewares with Oak by calling *app.use*.

In our example, *app.use* receives the middleware function:

```
app.use((ctx) => {
  ctx.response.body = "Hello World!";
});
```

The middleware receives a context object *ctx* that represents the current request. It contains useful properties like the request URL and request method etc. For example, if we add the below codes in **bold** to *app.ts*:

23

```
import { Application } from "https://deno.land/x/oak/mod.ts";

const app = new Application();

app.use((ctx) => {
  console.log(ctx.request.url);
  console.log(ctx.request.method);
  ctx.response.body = "Hello World!";
});

await app.listen({ port: 8000 });
```

and run your app with:

```
deno run --allow-net app.ts
```

When you go to your browser, you will see 'Hello World!'. In the console, you will also see the request URL printed:

```
URL { href: "http://localhost:8000/", origin: "http://localhost:8000",
protocol: "http:", username: "", password: "", host: "localhost:8000",
hostname: "localhost", port: "8000", pathname: "/", hash: "", search:
"" }
```

and also the request method:

```
GET
```

Next, you decide what to return to the client with *ctx.response* e.g. `ctx.response.body = "Hello World!"`. We will see later how to use context for different use cases.

To recap, the Oak library automatically executes the middleware provided to *app.use* for every request.

Understanding Multiple Middleware Functions

In our current example, we only have one middleware. But in real-world applications, we will often have multiple middleware functions each doing different things. For instance, one middleware function extracts data from an incoming request and another middleware function prepares the response.

How do we use multiple middleware functions together? We illustrate with the following example. Add the following codes in **bold**:

```
import { Application } from "https://deno.land/x/oak/mod.ts";

const app = new Application();

app.use((ctx,next) => {
  console.log(ctx.request.url);
  console.log(ctx.request.method);
  ctx.response.body = "Hello World!";
  next();
});

app.use((ctx,next) => {
  console.log("middle ware 2");
  ctx.response.body = "Message from middleware 2";
});

await app.listen({ port: 8000 });
```

Notice that in the middleware, we now add a *next* argument. At the end of the first middleware, we call *next()*. This tells Oak that after this middleware, we want to forward the request to the next middleware below. That is, a request travels through middleware functions from top to bottom.
If we don't call *next*, the next middleware won't be reached, and the response will just be sent back.

In our example, the request reaches the second middleware and because there isn't a *next()*, it will end and sends back the response "Message from middleware 2" to the client.

So, if we quit the current program and run again:

```
deno run --allow-net app.ts
```

When we go to localhost:8000, we get "Message from middleware 2" in the browser and also "middle ware 2" logged in the console.

Automatic Server Restart with *denon*

We have been starting and stopping our server each time we make a code change in *app.ts*. Now, we will install a package called *denon* that automatically detects code changes and restart the server, so we don't have to stop and restart it manually. A similar tool for Node is *nodemon*.

As per the instructions in *https://deno.land/x/denon*, install *denon* with the commands they provide (fig. 4):

Install

To install denon simply enter the following into a terminal:

deno.land

```
$ deno install --allow-read --allow-run --allow-write --allow-net -f --unstable https://deno.land/x/denon@v2.3.0/denon.ts
```

nest.land

```
$ deno install --allow-read --allow-run --allow-write --allow-net -f --unstable https://x.nest.land/denon@2.3.0/denon.ts
```

⚠ Make sure you are using `deno` version `^1.2.0` to install this executable. You can upgrade running `deno` `upgrade`.

(Figure 4 – denon v2.3.0 at time of writing)

You should be able to run *denon* in your Terminal with:

```
denon run --allow-net app.ts
```

Now, each time you make a code change, *denon* will automatically detect it and restart the server.

Handling Requests with Oak

Oak allows great flexibility in responding to browser 'get' or 'post' requests using the *Router* object. To illustrate this, fill in *app.ts* with the following code:

```
import { Application, Router } from "https://deno.land/x/oak/mod.ts";

const app = new Application();
const router = new Router();
```

```
router.get('/',(ctx,next)=>{
    ctx.response.body = `<h1>The home page\n</h1>`
    ctx.response.type = 'text/html';
});

router.get('/about',(ctx,next)=>{
    ctx.response.body = `<h1>The about page\n</h1>`
    ctx.response.type = 'text/html';
});

router.get('/contact',(ctx,next)=>{
    ctx.response.body = `<h1>The contact page\n</h1>`
    ctx.response.type = 'text/html';
});

app.use(router.routes());
app.use(router.allowedMethods());

await app.listen({ port: 8000 });
```

Code Explanation

```
import { Application, Router } from "https://deno.land/x/oak/mod.ts";

const app = new Application();
const router = new Router();
```

Here, we import both the *Application* and *Router* construction functions. We have previously used the *Application* constructor. Here, we are introduced to the *Router* constructor function.

We create a *router* object with *new Router()*. *Router* has a method for every key HTTP method i.e. *router.get*, *router.post, router.put, router.delete* etc. These allows us to register routes for incoming HTTP requests. For example, to register a route for an incoming GET request with the path '/', i.e. *localhost:8000/* or *mydomain.com/* we have:

```
router.get('/',(ctx,next)=>{
    ctx.response.body = `<h1>The home page\n</h1>`;
    ctx.response.type = 'text/html';
});
```

That is, for every incoming request to *localhost:8000/*, the function in the second argument will be triggered. In the function, we respond with the body `<h1>The home page\n</h1>`.

Note that the HTML is wrapped with backticks `. This allows us to specify the HTML in multiple lines for example:

```
ctx.response.body = `
  <h1>
    The home page\n
    </h1>
  `;
```

To register a route for an incoming GET request with the path '/about', i.e. *localhost:8000/about*, we have:

```
router.get('/about',(ctx,next)=>{
    ctx.response.body = `<h1>The about page\n</h1>`
    ctx.response.type = 'text/html';
});
```

And similarly for the path '/contact', we have:

```
router.get('/contact',(ctx,next)=>{
    ctx.response.body = `<h1>The contact page\n</h1>`
    ctx.response.type = 'text/html';
});
```

Lastly, to inform Oak of our *router* middleware, we register it with *app.use*:

```
app.use(router.routes());
app.use(router.allowedMethods());
```

Running your App

When you run your app now, it will serve the *about* HTML markup when a request to */about* comes in and serve the *contact* markup when a request to */contact* comes in.

So, you can see that Oak through its *router* middleware helps us respond better to different browser requests paths and types. In the above, we handled HTTP GET requests with *route.get*. A GET request gets resources like a homepage, an image etc. It does not change the state of our app. Later, we illustrate handling POST, PATCH and DELETE requests that change the state of our app.

Routing

We have illustrated how we can define specific routes and its response our server gives when a route is hit. This is also called *Routing* where we map requests to specific handlers depending on their URL. Previously without Oak, we had to respond to individual routes with an extended *if-else* statement in one big request handler:

```
for await (const req of s) {
  const headers = new Headers();
  headers.set('Content-Type','text/html');
  if(req.url === '/about')
    req.respond({ body: "<h1>The about page</h1>", headers: headers });
  else if(req.url === '/contact')
    req.respond({ body: "<h1>The contact page</h1>", headers: headers });
  else if(req.url === '/')
    req.respond({ body: "<h1>The home page\n</h1>", headers: headers });
  else {
    req.respond({ body: "not found", headers: headers, status:404 });
  }
}
```

With Oak, we can refactor this big request handler into many smaller request handlers that each handles a specific route. This allows us to build our app in a more modular and maintainable way. Thus, I hope you come to slowly appreciate how Oak makes it easier to write these request handler functions and in general, simplify development in Deno.

However, we still have room to improve. Our HTML code is currently hard-coded. In a real app, we will have much more HTML than just short snippets like what we now have. To handle larger amounts of HTML efficiently and elegantly, we dive into templating engines in the next chapter.

Summary

In this chapter, we learned how to utilize third-party modules. A core third party module, Oak, helps make it easier to handle different kinds of requests and serve responses via the *Router* object. We were introduced to the concept of middlewares. We improved our development experience by having automatic server restarts upon code changes with *denon*. In the next chapter, we will learn about templating engines to help dynamically render HTML pages.

Refer to https://github.com/greglim81/deno_chapter2 for the source code of this chapter. If you face any issues, contact me at support@i-ducate.com.

Chapter 3: Introducing Templating Engines

In a real world app, a lot of code we send back to the client contains dynamic data e.g. data fetched from a database. We don't always return the same HTML page. Instead, we return the same HTML skeleton but with different data depending on the user. For example, what we see on amazon.com differs for each user.

The skeleton, header, footer of the site might be the same, but the data fetched for each user is different. So, we can't just store HTML files on the server and send them. Instead, we need templates which are basically HTML pages with specific custom templating language inside of it. The template is then parsed dynamically by Deno to render actual data in those placeholders. In essence, templating engines help us dynamically render HTML pages in contrast to just having fixed static pages.

For example, in HTML you might have:

```
<h1>All Todos</h1>
<ul>
  … <!--dynamic data to be fetched from database-->
</ul>
```

In a template, we have templating code injecting into the HTML to render dynamic data. It would look something like:

```
<h1>All Todos</h1>
<ul>
    <% for (let i = 0; i < todos.length; i++){ %>
    <li><%= todos[i].name %></li>
    <% } %>
</ul>
```

Using the EJS Templating Engine

EJS is a popular templating engine in Node as well as Deno. As stated on its site (fig. 1), EJS is a simple templating language that lets us generate HTML with plain JavaScript in simple straightforward scriptlet tags `<%= … %>`.

31

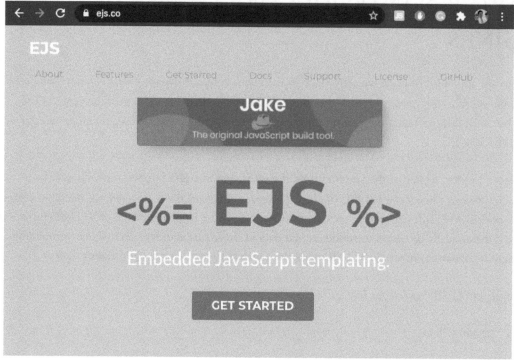

Figure 1

There are many templating engines out there like Handlebars, Pug, and more. But we will use 'EJS' (which stands for Embedded JavaScript) because it is one of the more popular templating engines and is made by the people who created Deno. All these different templating engines at the end of the day have the same purpose which is to output HTML. When you understand one, you mostly know how to use another.

To begin using EJS in our Deno project, from the project in the previous chapter, in *app.ts*, add the following in bold:

```
import { Application, Router } from "https://deno.land/x/oak/mod.ts";
import { renderFileToString } from
'https://deno.land/x/dejs@0.8.0/mod.ts';

const app = new Application();

const router = new Router();
```

```
router.get('/',async (ctx,next)=>{
    const body = await renderFileToString(Deno.cwd()+'/todos.ejs',{title:
'My Todos'});
    ctx.response.body = body;
});

app.use(router.routes());
app.use(router.allowedMethods());

await app.listen({ port: 8000 });
```

Code Explanation

```
import {renderFileToString} from 'https://deno.land/x/dejs@0.8.0/mod.ts';
```

To use EJS, we make us of the third-party module *dejs* (no prizes for guessing what 'dejs' stands for). We import `renderFileToString` from *dejs* which takes an *ejs* file and convert it to a string that we can set as our response body later.

```
router.get('/',async (ctx,next)=>{
    const body = await renderFileToString(Deno.cwd()+'/todos.ejs',{title:
'My Todos'});
    ctx.response.body = body;
});
```

`renderFileToString` takes in two arguments. The first being the file path of the ejs file and the second being the params object we feed to the ejs file. We specify `{title: 'My Todos'}` as the params object. In it, we have the property *title* with the value 'My Todos'.

Because `renderFileToString` returns a *Promise<String>*, we specify *await* before it. In doing so, we also specify *async* in the function header.

Because we are using *dejs*, Oak can auto determine the response type and we don't have to specify *ctx.response.type = 'text/html'* as what we have done before.

We will later create our own ejs file *todos.ejs* in the same directory as *app.ts*. We first specify the path as `Deno.cwd()+'/todos.ejs'`. *Deno.cwd* returns us the current working directory where *app.ts* is stored.

33

todos.ejs

Now let's proceed to create a new file *todos.ejs* in our folder. Note that the filetype has to be '.ejs'. To auto-generate a standard HTML5 template in VSCode, in *todos.ejs*, type *html:5* (fig. 2)

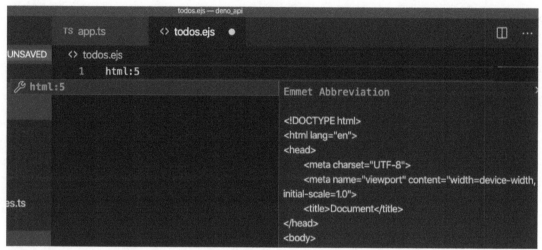

Figure 2

And you will have the following HTML generated for you.

```
<!DOCTYPE html>
<html lang="en">
<head>
    <meta charset="UTF-8">
    <meta name="viewport" content="width=device-width, initial-
scale=1.0">
    <title>Document</title>
</head>
<body>
</body>
</html>
```

Make the changes in **bold**:

```
<!DOCTYPE html>
<html lang="en">
<head>
    <meta charset="UTF-8">
    <meta name="viewport" content="width=device-width, initial-
scale=1.0">
    <title><%= title %></title>
</head>
<body>
    <h1><%= title %></h1>
</body>
</html>
```

As you can see, an *ejs* file is simply a HTML file except that it has special tags *<% %>* for us to insert our templating code. In the above, we have **<%= title %>** inserted into the *<title>* and *<body>* tags. Remember the 2nd param object we passed into:

```
const body = await renderFileToString(Deno.cwd()+'/todos.ejs',
            {title: 'My Todos'});
```

<%= title %> will refer to the *title* property that is passed in and render "My Todos".

Running your App

Run the app with:

```
denon run --allow-net --allow-read app.ts
```

Note that we have to add the **--allow-read** permission to allow *renderFileToString* to read files. If we don't specify this, we will get an error. And when you go the localhost:8000/, you will see "My Todos" rendered in the browser (fig. 3).

My Todos

Figure 3

Rendering Lists of Data

We have successfully dynamically rendered *title* in our *ejs* page. But how do we render lists of data for e.g. in figure 4?

My Todos

- Learn Deno
- Prepare lunch
- Read bible

Figure 4

To do so, add the following codes in **bold** into *app.ts*:

```
...
const app = new Application();
const router = new Router();

const todos: {id: String, name: String }[] = [
    {id: "1",name: "Learn Deno"},
    {id: "2",name: "Prepare lunch"},
    {id: "3",name: "Read bible"}
];

router.get('/',async (ctx,next)=>{
    const body = await renderFileToString(Deno.cwd()+'/todos.ejs',{
        title: 'My Todos',
        todos: todos
    });
    ctx.response.body = body;
```

```
});
...
```

Code Explanation

```
const todos: {id: String, name: String }[] = [
    {id: "1",name: "Learn Deno"},
    {id: "2",name: "Prepare lunch"},
    {id: "3",name: "Read bible"}
];
```

We instantiate a *todos* array of three todo objects. Each todo object consists of an id and a name.

```
router.get('/',async (ctx,next)=>{
    const body = await renderFileToString(Deno.cwd()+'/todos.ejs',{
        title: 'My Todos',
        todos: todos
    });
    ctx.response.body = body;
});
```

We then pass *todos* into the template by specifying it in the params object.

todos.ejs

And in *todos.ejs*, we loop through *todos* and render each todo with the code in **bold**:

```
...
<body>
    <h1><%= title %></h1>
    <ul>
        <% for (let i = 0; i < todos.length; i++){ %>
         <li><%= todos[i].name %></li>
        <% } %>
    </ul>
</body>
</html>
```

If you run your app now, you should be able to see your todos rendered (fig. 5). And this is how we use Deno and EJS to render dynamic content.

My Todos

- Learn Deno
- Prepare lunch
- Read bible

Figure 5

Handling Errors

Now, what happens if I have a typo in my code:

```
<% for (let i = 0; i < todos.length; i++){ %>
 <li><%= todos[i].name %></li>
<% s} %>
```

For example, in the above, I accidentally add a 's' before closing the *for* loop. How can I be notified that there is my error in code?

We can add a middleware that *try*, *catch* any error and runs before other middlewares. Add the following to *app.ts*:

```
...
app.use(async (ctx,next) =>{
    try{
      await next();
    }
    catch(err){
        console.log(err);
    }
});

app.use(router.routes());
app.use(router.allowedMethods());

await app.listen({ port: 8000 });
```

38

The newly added middleware doesn't really do anything except that it runs first and then awaits for the successive asynchronous middlewares to run and complete. Following which, it will return to this first middleware to the line after *next()*.

Essentially, this first middleware wraps the other intermediate middlewares by starting before the rest, awaits for them to finish, and then finishes last. In doing so, we wrap a try-catch block around this chain of middlewares and catch any errors that might occur.

So, if we run the app now, we get an error logged in the console:

error: Uncaught ReferenceError: s is not defined

We can then look into *todos.ejs* and look for '*s*'. We will revisit error handling later.

Summary

In this chapter, we learned about the EJS templating engine to help us dynamically render HTML pages in contrast to just having fixed static pages. We learned how to pass data into the templates and render them in a list. In the next chapter, we look at styling our app's user interface to make it look better.

Refer to https://github.com/greglim81/deno_chapter3 for the source code of this chapter. If you face any issues, contact me at support@i-ducate.com.

CHAPTER 4: STYLING A USER INTERFACE

Our page is looking rather plain at the moment. As this book is not about website design, CSS or how to come up with a graphical user interface, we will use components from *getbootstrap.com* to design a more professional looking UI.

To use Bootstrap, in the project from the previous chapter, copy-paste the stylesheet link from *https://getbootstrap.com/docs/4.5/getting-started/introduction/* into the <head> of *todos.ejs* to load its CSS. The link should look something like:

```
<link rel="stylesheet"
href=https://stackpath.bootstrapcdn.com/bootstrap/4.5.0/css/bootstrap.min.css…>
```

Next, we use the list group component (https://getbootstrap.com/docs/4.5/components/list-group/ - fig. 1) to list our todos.

Basic example

The most basic list group is an unordered list with list items and the proper classes.
Build upon it with the options that follow, or with your own CSS as needed.

Cras justo odio

Dapibus ac facilisis in

Morbi leo risus

Porta ac consectetur ac

Vestibulum at eros

Figure 1

Here is a sample markup from the site:

```
<ul class="list-group">
  <li class="list-group-item">Cras justo odio</li>
  <li class="list-group-item">Dapibus ac facilisis in</li>
  <li class="list-group-item">Morbi leo risus</li>
  <li class="list-group-item">Porta ac consectetur ac</li>
```

```
  <li class="list-group-item">Vestibulum at eros</li>
</ul>
```

To incorporate this into *todos.ejs*, add the following in **bold**:

```
...
<body>
    <h1><%= title %></h1>
    <ul class="list-group">
        <% for (let i = 0; i < todos.length;i++){ %>
         <li class="list-group-item"><%= todos[i].name %></li>
        <% } %>
    </ul>
</body>
</html>
```

And when we go to our browser, our todo app now displays the list of todos (fig. 2):

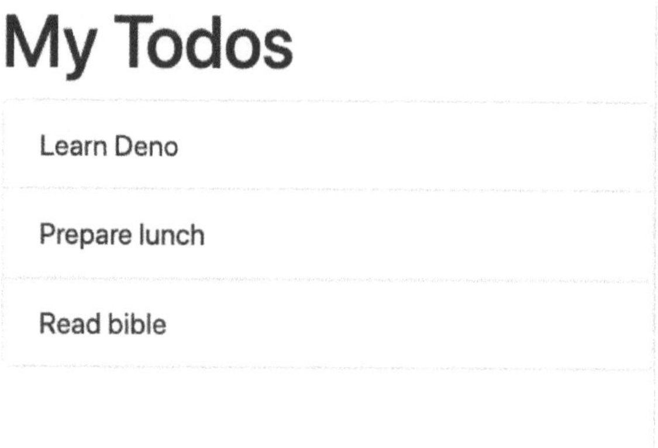

My Todos

Learn Deno

Prepare lunch

Read bible

Figure 2

Adding a Form to Add Todos

Now, let's add a simple form on the top of the list to add todos.

We will use inline forms (https://getbootstrap.com/docs/4.5/components/forms/#inline-forms). In *todos.ejs*, add the form with the code in **bold** below:

```
<body>
```

42

```
<h1><%= title %></h1>
<form class="form-inline">
    <input type="text" class="form-control mb-2 mr-sm-2">
    <button type="submit" class="btn btn-primary mb-2">
        Add Todo
    </button>
</form>
<ul class="list-group" >
    <% for (let i = 0; i < todos.length;i++){ %>
     <li class="list-group-item"><%= todos[i].name %></li>
    <% } %>
</ul>
</body>
```

And we get something like in figure 3:

My Todos

Figure 3

Form Request to Add Todos

To add a todo, a request should be sent when a user submits the form. To do so, add the below *action* and *method* property in <form>:

```
<form class="form-inline" action='/add-todo' method="POST">
  <input type="text" class="form-control mb-2 mr-sm-2" name="new-todo">
    <button type="submit" class="btn btn-primary mb-2">
      Add Todo
    </button>
```

43

```
</form>
```

With this, when our form submits, a request will be sent to the /add-todo route and that request will use the *POST* http method. A 'POST' request is needed to pass form data from the browser to our Deno app to create the record.

app.ts

We then need to handle this POST request to /add-todo in *app.ts*. Add the below *router.post* route in *app.ts*:

```
router.post('/add-todo',async (ctx,next) => {
    ...
});
```

Now, how do we extract the value entered into the 'new-todo' field? Add the following:

```
router.post('/add-todo',async (ctx,next) => {
  const newTodoTitle =  (await ctx.request.body({type:
"form"}).value).get('new-todo');
  console.log(newTodoTitle);
});
```

First, we specify that the body-type is a 'form' (we will later explore other types like *json* in a later chapter) and we get the form data from the browser via the request *body* attribute. *body* parses the incoming request body.

We use *await* upon **ctx.request.body({type: "form"}).value** as it returns us a Promise. We then specify the name of the input 'new-todo' which we want to get data from.

Note: Here, we handle a POST request which is generally used to request an addition to the state of the server unlike GET where we simply get resources. A user POSTs a blog entry, a photo, signing up for an account, buying an item etc. We explore later handling other types of requests for example, PATCH requests for modifying existing records.

With the retrieved input values, let's then proceed to create the todo object. To ensure that we don't add todos when the field is left blank, we add the *if* clause:

```
router.post('/add-todo',async (ctx,next) => {
```

```
        const newTodoTitle =  (await ctx.request.body({type:
"form"}).value).get('new-todo');

    if(newTodoTitle && newTodoTitle.trim().length !== 0){
        ...
    }
```

The *if* clause checks that *newTodoTitle* is not null and does not consist of just whitespaces. *trim* removes extra whitespaces at the beginning and end. So, if a user enters a bunch of whitespaces, the value is treated as invalid. We check that the length after the trimming is not 0 to ensure an empty todo is not accepted.

```
if(newTodoTitle && newTodoTitle.trim().length !== 0){
        //new todo object
        const newTodo = {
            id: new Date().toISOString(),
            name: newTodoTitle!
        };
        todos.push(newTodo);
        console.log(newTodo);
        ctx.response.redirect('/')
    }
```

In the *if*-clause, we then create a new todo object *newTodo*. We use the datetime stamp as an id for now. This is not ideal because we might have two users concurrently creating a todo at the same time. But later when we use MongoDB, we will replace this with the id that they generate for us.

We then push *newTodo* into *todos*. And redirect the user to the main page.

The entire *router.post('/add-todo')* should look like:

```
router.post('/add-todo',async (ctx,next) => {
    const newTodoTitle =  (await ctx.request.body({type:
"form"}).value).get('new-todo');

    if(newTodoTitle && newTodoTitle.trim().length !== 0){
        const newTodo = {
            id: new Date().toISOString(),
            name: newTodoTitle!
        };
```

```
        todos.push(newTodo);
        console.log(newTodo);
        ctx.response.redirect('/')
    }
});
```

Running your App

When you run your app now, you will be able to add new todos (fig. 4).

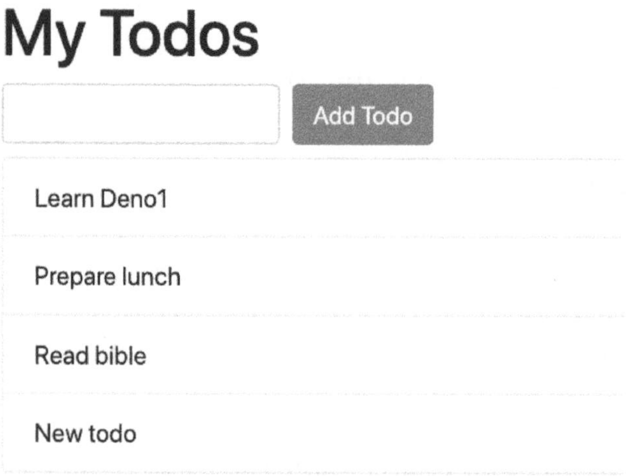

My Todos

	Add Todo

Learn Deno1

Prepare lunch

Read bible

New todo

Figure 4

Showing Warnings

But what should we do if a user enters a blank value and hits on 'Add Todo'? We should highlight with a warning that the field cannot be empty. Let's do this by adding the below *else* clause in **bold**:

```
router.post('/add-todo',async (ctx,next) => {
    const newTodoTitle =  (await ctx.request.body({type:
"form"}).value).get('new-todo');

    if(newTodoTitle && newTodoTitle.trim().length !== 0){
        ...
    }
    else{
```

46

```
        const body = await renderFileToString(Deno.cwd()+'/todos.ejs',{
            title: 'My Todos',
            todos: todos,
            error: "Field cannot be empty"
        });
        ctx.response.body = body;
    }
});
```

That is, we render *todos.ejs* with an added *error* property with the value "Field cannot be empty".

And back in *todos.ejs*, just after *<form>* and before **<ul class="list-group" >**, we add the error alert with the below **codes** in bold:

```
<body>
    <h1><%= title %></h1>
    <form class="form-inline" action='/add-todo' method="POST">

      ...
    </form>
    <% if (error) { %>
        <div class="alert alert-danger" role="alert">
            <%= error %>
        </div>
    <% } %>
    <ul class="list-group" >
        <% for (let i = 0; i < todos.length;i++){ %>
         <li class="list-group-item"><%= todos[i].name %></li>
        <% } %>
    </ul>
</body>
```

It will check if the *error* property has a value and if it does, render the *error* message. And because we check for *error* in *todos.ejs*, we also have to add it in our *route.get*:

```
router.get('/',async (ctx,next)=>{
    const body = await renderFileToString(Deno.cwd()+'/todos.ejs',{
        title: 'My Todos',
        todos: todos,
        error: null
    });
    ctx.response.body = body;
```

```
});
```

Only this time, we specify that *error* is null. Thus the error warning will not be displayed.

When we run our app now and try to add a todo with an empty field, we get (fig. 5):

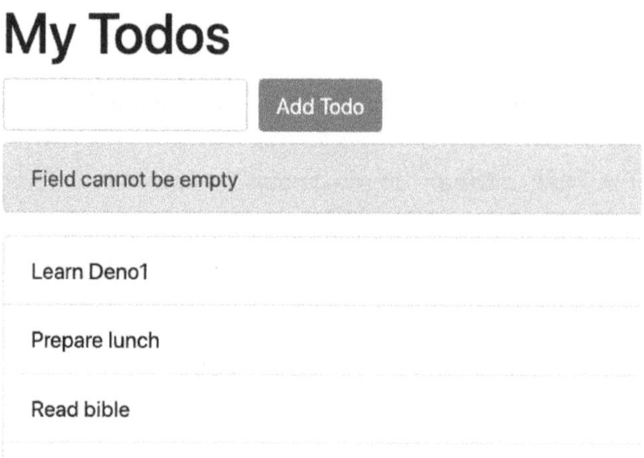

My Todos

Figure 5

We ensured that a user can add a todo only when they enter a value. With this, we have illustrated how you can do simple form validation and show error warnings back to the user. Can you come with more of your own custom validation checks and render them to the user? For e.g. todo length should be more three characters.

Summary

We utilized *getbootstrap* to design a more professional looking user interface. We added a form to add todos and sends a POST request which we handle in our routes. We also implemented a simple validation check which alerts the user for invalid inputs.

Now, our app files are getting larger. How do we make them more organized and manageable? We explore that in the next chapter.

Refer to https://github.com/greglim81/deno_chapter4 for the source code of this chapter. If you face any issues, contact me at support@i-ducate.com.

CHAPTER 5: RE-STRUCTURING OUR APP

So far, the code for our todo app is contained in just two files, *app.ts* and *todos.ejs*. But in bigger apps, we ought to split code across multiple files to keep them more organized and manageable. Each file is kept lean and manageable on its own. This makes it easy to find what you are looking for and don't have to scroll through large files.

A common folder structure is to have a separate folder called *routes* to hold our routing logic. So, in your project folder, create a new folder 'routes'. And in it, create a file *todo-routes.ts* (fig. 1).

Figure 1

We will now move our routes out of *app.ts* into */routes/todo-routes.ts*. That is, *todo-routes.ts* should contain the following:

```
import { Router } from "https://deno.land/x/oak/mod.ts";
import { renderFileToString } from
'https://deno.land/x/dejs@0.8.0/mod.ts';//

const router = new Router();

const todos: {id: String, name: String }[] = [
    {id: "1",name: "Learn Deno1"},
    {id: "2",name: "Prepare lunch"},
    {id: "3",name: "Read bible"}
];

router.get('/',async (ctx,next)=>{
    const body = await renderFileToString(Deno.cwd()+'/todos.ejs',{
        title: 'My Todos',
        todos: todos,
        error: null
    });
```

```
        ctx.response.body = body;
});

router.post('/add-todo',async (ctx,next) => {
    const newTodoTitle =  (await ctx.request.body({type:
"form"}).value).get('new-todo');

    if(newTodoTitle && newTodoTitle.trim().length !== 0){
        const newTodo ={
            id: new Date().toISOString(),
            name: newTodoTitle!
        };
        todos.push(newTodo);
        console.log(newTodo);
        ctx.response.redirect('/')
    }
    else{
        const body = await renderFileToString(Deno.cwd()+'/todos.ejs',{
            title: 'My Todos',
            todos: todos,
            error: "Field cannot be empty"
        });
        ctx.response.body = body;
    }
});

export default router;
```

Note that we have added *export default router* in *todos-routes.ts* because *app.ts* requires access to it.

app.ts

And back in *app.ts*, we need to import *router* with:

```
import { Application } from "https://deno.land/x/oak/mod.ts";
import router from "./routes/todo-routes.ts";

const app = new Application();

app.use(async (ctx,next) =>{
    try{
```

```
      await next();
   }
   catch(err){
      console.log(err);
      ctx.response.body = "Something went wrong. Please try again
later.";
   }
});
app.use(router.routes());
app.use(router.allowedMethods());
await app.listen({ port: 8000 });
```

The rest of the code in *app.ts* remains unchanged. But note how leaner *app.ts* is now that the routes have been organized into another file.

Templates

Currently, we have only one templating file *todos.ejs*. But this would most definitely grow as our app grows. To facilitate this, we will put our templates in a separate *views* folder. So, in the project folder, create a new *views* folder and move *todos.ejs* into it.

We then have to update the paths referring to *todos.ejs*. In *todo-routes.ts*, there are two lines of code which refer to *todos.ejs*. Add 'views' to the path for example:

```
const body = await renderFileToString(Deno.cwd()+'/views/todos.ejs',{
```

If we run our app now, it should run fine as before. Except that now, we have organized our app better into *views* and *routes* folders. This will form the foundation of having our app patterned after the MVC architecture. We will come to MVC later.

Summary

In this chapter, we split our code across different folders (*routes*, *views*) and files to keep them more organized and manageable. Each file is kept lean and manageable on its own. This makes it easy to find what you are looking for and don't have to scroll through large files.

In the next chapter, we will look at a core concept for any app, C.R.U.D. operations.

Refer to https://github.com/greglim81/deno_chapter5 for the source code of this chapter. If you face any issues, contact me at support@i-ducate.com.

CHAPTER 6: IMPLEMENTING C.R.U.D. OPERATIONS

We will look at a core concept core of any web app, C.R.U.D. which stands for Create, Read, Update and Delete. We have actually implemented create and read in our todo app.

Let's go on to implement delete. To delete a todo, we will send a POST request together with the id of the todo to be deleted. You might be asking, shouldn't we be sending a DELETE request since it's a delete operation? That is because we typically use a POST request for deleting from a web app unless we are building a REST API. It is a convention to use POST for deleting because we are manipulating something on the server.

So, in *todo-routes.ts*, we handle the delete request by adding the route:

```
router.post('/delete-todo/:todoId', (ctx) => {
    const id = ctx.params.todoId;
    todos = todos.filter(todo => todo.id !== id);
    ctx.response.redirect('/');
});
```

Code Explanation

/delete-todo/:todoId in the route is a placeholder for the id of the todo we want to delete. So, the URL request to delete a todo will be something like *mydomain.com/delete-todo/1* where *todoId* is '1'.

```
    const id = ctx.params.todoId;
```

The context object *ctx*, has a *params* object that contains *todoId* passed into the route placeholder.

```
    todos = todos.filter(todo => todo.id !== id);
```

The *todos* array has a *filter* method that takes in a function which executes on every element in the array. If the function returns true, we keep the element. If it returns false, we drop it. *filter* then finally returns a brand-new array with the new set of filtered elements. So, with *todo.id !== id*, we get a new array but without that specified todo to be deleted.

53

Now because we are altering our *todos* array, we need to change the declaration of *todos* from: **const** *todos* to **let** *todos*.

Adding a Delete Button

Now that we have the delete route, let's add the delete button to remove a todo. In *todos.ejs*, add the following in **bold**:

```
<ul class="list-group" >
    <% for (let i = 0; i < todos.length;i++){ %>
     <li class="list-group-item
        d-flex justify-content-between align-items-center">
        <%= todos[i].name %>
        <form action='/delete-todo/<%= todos[i].id %>' method="POST">
            <button type="submit"
              class="btn btn-primary mb-2">Delete</button>
        </form>
     </li>
    <% } %>
</ul>
```

Code Explanation

```
<li class="list-group-item
    d-flex justify-content-between align-items-center">
```

We first justify and align the todo item and button.

```
<form action='/delete-todo/<%= todos[i].id %>' method="POST">
    <button type="submit"
      class="btn btn-primary mb-2">Delete</button>
</form>
```

We then add a form with a Delete button to trigger a POST request to */delete-todo/:todoId*. In *action*, we render the todo's id together with the *delete-todo* route.

Running our App

Our app should look something like where we will be able to delete todos (fig. 1).

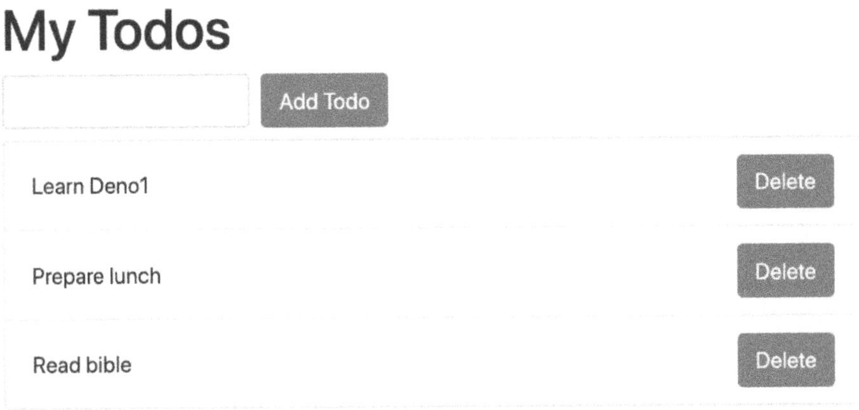

My Todos

Figure 1

Retrieving a Specific Todo

Before we implement updating a todo, a user has to first click on an existing todo, and then she will be brought to that todo's details page for the update. We thus need the route to retrieve a specific todo.

In *todo-routes.ts*, add:

```
router.get('/todo/:todoId', async (ctx) => {
    const id = ctx.params.todoId;

    const todo = todos.find(todo => todo.id === id);
    if(!todo){
      throw new Error('did not find todo')
    }
    const body = await renderFileToString(Deno.cwd()+'/views/todo.ejs',{
      todoText: todo.name,
      todoId: todo.id,
      error: null
    });

    ctx.response.body = body;
});
```

Code Explanation

```
router.get('/todo/:todoId'
```

Like the route for deleting a specific todo, we specify in the route */todo/:todoId* a placeholder for the id of the todo to retrieve. The URL request to retrieve a todo will be something like *mydomain.com/todo/1* with request type 'GET' (since we are not making any changes but just retrieving data for now).

```
const id = ctx.params.todoId;
```

We extract *todoId* from the params object.

```
const todo = todos.find(todo => todo.id === id);
```

todos array has a built-in *find* method which takes in a function that is executed on every element in the array, and returns the todo for which the function returns true, i.e. *todo.id == id.*

In the event that a user manually enters the route into the browser e.g. *mydomain.com/todo/<somestring>* and that id doesn't exist in todos, we should throw an error to prevent our app from crashing. We thus check if *todo* is null. And if so, throw an error:

```
if(!todo){
   throw new Error('did not find todo')
}
```

When the error is thrown, the execution of the function will stop and be caught in the first middleware *catch* clause.

```
const body = await renderFileToString(Deno.cwd()+'/views/todo.ejs',{
   todoText: todo.name,
   todoId: todo.id,
   error: null
});
```

We then render the todo detail page *todo.ejs* (we will implement it later) and pass in the todo's name and id properties. We also pass in a null for the *error* property. Similar to the error warning displayed when adding todos, *error* will be used to display error warnings if any in *todo.ejs* when updating a todo.

56

To generate *todo.ejs*, we can make a copy of *todos.ejs* and remove its <ul class="list-group" > component.

It should look something like below but note the changes in **bold**:

todo.ejs

```
<!DOCTYPE html>
<html lang="en">
<head>
    <meta charset="UTF-8">
    <meta name="viewport" …>
    <title><%= todoText %></title>
    <link rel="stylesheet"
href="https://stackpath.bootstrapcdn.com/bootstrap/4.5.0/css/bootstrap.min.css"
integrity="sha384-
9aIt2nRpC12Uk9gS9baDl411NQApFmC26EwAOH8WgZl5MYYxFfc+NcPb1dKGj7Sk"
crossorigin="anonymous">
</head>
<body>
    <h1><%= todoText %></h1>
    <form class="form-inline" action='/update-todo/ <%= todoId %>' method="POST">
        <input type="text"
                class="form-control mb-2 mr-sm-2"
                name="update-todo"
                value="<%= todoText %>"
         >
        <button type="submit" class="btn btn-primary mb-2">Update Todo</button>
    </form>
    <% if (error) { %>
        <div class="alert alert-danger" role="alert">
            <%= error %>
        </div>
    <% } %>
</body>
</html>
```

Code Explanation

```
    <h1><%= todoText %></h1>
```

Just as in *todos.ejs*, we inject *todoText* in the <title> and in <h1> of <body>.

```
    <form class="form-inline" action='/update-todo/ <%= todoId %>' method="POST">
```

In <form>, we set the route in action to /*update-todo*/ <%= *todoId* %> which we later handle in *todo-routes.ts*.

```
<input type="text"
       class="form-control mb-2 mr-sm-2"
       name="update-todo"
       value="<%= todoText %>"
   >
```

With the above, we inject *todoText* into the 'update-todo' field's *value* to pre-populate the field with the existing todo.

todos.ejs

Lastly, in *todos.ejs*, we wrap each <li> row in `<a href="/<%= todos[i].id %>">` as shown below in **bold**:

```
<ul class="list-group" >
    <% for (let i = 0; i < todos.length;i++){ %>
    <a href="/todo/<%= todos[i].id %>">
        <li class="list-group-item
                d-flex justify-content-between align-items-center">
            <%= todos[i].name %>
            <form action='/delete-todo/<%= todos[i].id %>' method="POST">
                <button type="submit" class="btn btn-primary mb-2">
                    Delete
                </button>
            </form>
        </li>
    </a>
    <% } %>
</ul>
```

With this, each time we click on a *todo* row, it will trigger the specific todo route `/todo/:todoId` in a GET request. This will be handled by `router.get('/todo/:todoId'` we defined earlier.

Running your App

When you run your app, your todos will be listed as links (fig. 2). Each todo has a link of

58

mydomain.com/todo/todoId.

My Todos

	Add Todo

Learn Deno1	Delete

Prepare lunch	Delete

Read bible	Delete

Figure 2

When you click on any of them, you will be brought to that todo's detail page where you can update it (fig. 3).

Prepare lunch

Prepare lunch	Update Todo

Figure 3

And if we enter an invalid *todoId* in the browser, we get the error "Something went wrong. Please try again later." because we threw the error back in *todo-routes.ts*:

```
router.get('/todo/:todoId', async (ctx) => {
    const id = ctx.params.todoId;
    const todo = todos.find(todo => todo.id === id);
    if(!todo){
      throw new Error('did not find todo')
    }
    ...
```

Now, let's go ahead to implement update.

Updating a Todo

Because our update todo form's action points to `/update-todo/ <%= todoId %>`:

```
<form class="form-inline" action='/update-todo/<%= todoId %>'
```

In *todo-routes.ts*, we add the route handler:

```
router.post('/update-todo/:todoId', async (ctx) => {
    const id = ctx.params.todoId;

    const todo = todos.find(todo => todo.id === id);
    if(!todo){
        throw new Error('did not find todo')
    }

    const updatedTodoTitle = (await ctx.request.body({type:
"form"}).value).get('update-todo');

    if(updatedTodoTitle && updatedTodoTitle.trim().length !== 0){
        todo.name = updatedTodoTitle;
        ctx.response.redirect('/')
    }
    else{
        const body = await
renderFileToString(Deno.cwd()+'/views/todo.ejs',{
            todoText: todo.name,
            todoId: todo.id,
            error: "Field cannot be empty"
        });
        ctx.response.body = body;
    }
});
```

Code Explanation

Much of the code would be familiar to you as we have gone through similar code earlier.

```
if(!todo){
    throw new Error('did not find todo')
}
```

We extract id from the route placeholder (`const id = ctx.params.todoId;`) and try to find the todo with that id (`todos.find(todo => todo.id === id);`). If the id cannot be found, (perhaps a user manually enters the route into the browser), we throw an error.

```
const updatedTodoTitle = (await ctx.request.body({type:
"form"}).value).get('update-todo');
```

We then retrieve the newly entered todo title.

```
if(updatedTodoTitle && updatedTodoTitle.trim().length !== 0){
    todo.name = updatedTodoTitle;
    ctx.response.redirect('/')
}
```

We assign the updated todo title to the retrieved todo object and redirect back to the home page.

```
const body = await
renderFileToString(Deno.cwd()+'/views/todo.ejs',{
        todoText: todo.name,
        todoId: todo.id,
        error: "Field cannot be empty"
    });
    ctx.response.body = body;
}
```

If the user enters a blank value or just whitespaces, we redirect them back to *todo.js* but with a warning message 'Field cannot be empty' in *error* property just as we did when adding a todo.

Running our App

You will be able to update todos now. And if the user enters in a blank value or just whitespaces, we get a warning message (fig. 4):

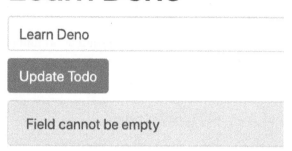

Figure 4

With this, we now have Create, Read, Update and Delete operations in place. But so far, we have been storing our data locally in an array and our data is lost when the program shuts down. In the next chapter, we will look at how we can get our Deno app to interact with a database to keep our data persistent.

Refer to https://github.com/greglim81/deno_chapter6 for the source code of this chapter. If you face any issues, contact me at support@i-ducate.com.

CHAPTER 7: USING MONGODB AS OUR DATABASE

We have been storing our data locally in an array. But because we are not using permanent storage, the data is lost when the program shuts down. In this chapter, we will look at how we can get our Deno app to interact with a database to keep our data persistent. We illustrate this with one of the most popular database storage, MongoDB. You can of course use other solutions to persist your application data e.g. in files, in a relational SQL database, or in another kind of storage mechanism.

If you have used Node before, you probably do not need any introduction to MongoDB. But for those who are unfamiliar with it, MongoDB is a NoSQL database. Before we talk about what is a NoSQL database, let's first talk about relational databases so that we can provide a meaningful contrast. If you have not heard of a relational database before, you can think of relational databases like spreadsheets where data is structured and each entry is generally a row in a table. Relational databases are generally controlled with SQL or Structured Query Language. Examples of popular relational databases are MySQL, SQL Server and PostgreSQL.

NoSQL databases are often called non-relational databases, where NoSQL means anything that isn't an SQL (see how it infers the popularity of SQL?). It might seem like NoSQL is a protest over SQL but it actually refers to a database not structured like a spreadsheet, i.e. less rigid than SQL databases.

So, why use MongoDB? Firstly, it is popular and that means there is plenty of help online. Secondly, it is mature being around since 2007 and used by companies like eBay, Craigslist and Orange.

Architecture of MongoDB

MongoDB stores information in the form of *collections* and *documents*. A *collection* represents a single entity in our app, for example in an e-commerce app, we need entities like categories, users, products. Each of these entity will be a single *collection* in our database.

A *collection* then contains *documents*. A *document* is an instance of the entity containing the various relevant fields to represent the *document*. For example, a product *document* will contain name, image and price fields. Each field is a key-value pair. Documents look a lot like JSON objects with various properties (though they are technically Binary JSON or BSON). An example of a collection-document tree is shown below:

```
Database
  → Products collection
      → Product document
            {
               price: 26,
               title: "Learning Deno",
               description: "Top Notch Development book",
               expiry date: 27-3-2022
            }
      → Product document
      ...
  → Users collection
      → User document
            {
               username: "123xyz",
               contact:
                   {
                      phone: "123-456-7890",
                      email: "xyz@example.com"
                   }
            }
      → User document
      ...
```

Setting Up MongoDB

There are a couple of ways to install MongoDB. You can install and launch a MongoDB server on your local machine. But in this book, we will use its cloud-based service MongoDB Atlas which will also put us in better stead to release our app to the world.

First, sign up for a MongoDB Atlas account (https://www.mongodb.com/cloud/atlas - fig. 1) and login.

MongoDB Atlas

Move faster with a cloud MongoDB service. Built for agile teams who'd rather spend time building apps than managing databases. Available on AWS, Azure, and GCP.

Already have an account? Log in here →

Figure 1

Select 'Create a New Cluster' (fig. 2)

Create a cluster

Choose your cloud provider, region, and specs.

Build a Cluster

Once your cluster is up and running, live migrate an existing MongoDB database into Atlas with our Live Migration Service.

Figure 2

Next, select the free 'Shared Clusters' option (fig. 3).

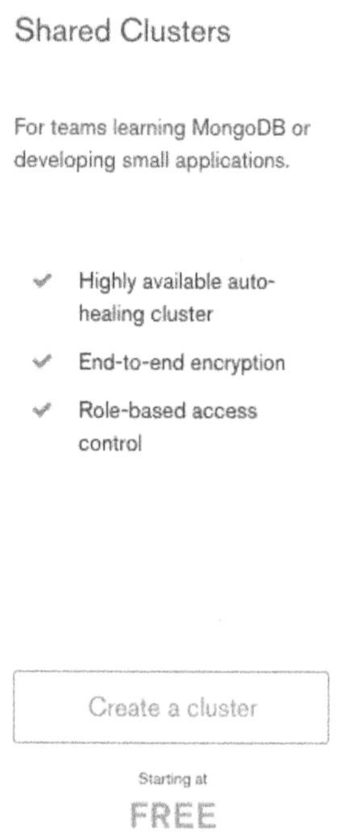

Shared Clusters

For teams learning MongoDB or
developing small applications.

- ✔ Highly available auto-
  healing cluster
- ✔ End-to-end encryption
- ✔ Role-based access
  control

Create a cluster

Starting at
FREE

Figure 3

You will be brought to a 'Create New Cluster' page. Under 'Global Cluster Configuration', choose 'AWS' as cloud provider (because they provide a free account without having to enter credit card details). Under 'North America', select 'North Virginia' where we can get a free tier for our MongoDB (fig. 4).

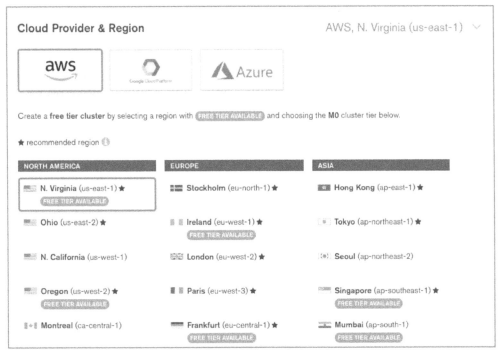

Figure 4

Next under 'Cluster Tier', choose the 'M0' free tier (fig. 5).

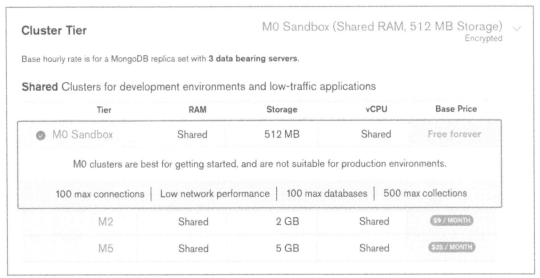

Figure 5

The good thing about Amazon AWS is that we can experiment without having to worry about making unintentional mistakes and getting a huge bill from Amazon. When your website gets more popular with more users, you can then scale up at a later stage. Keep the other default options and select 'Create Cluster.' It will prompt you saying that it takes 7-10 minutes to set up everything on AWS (fig. 6).

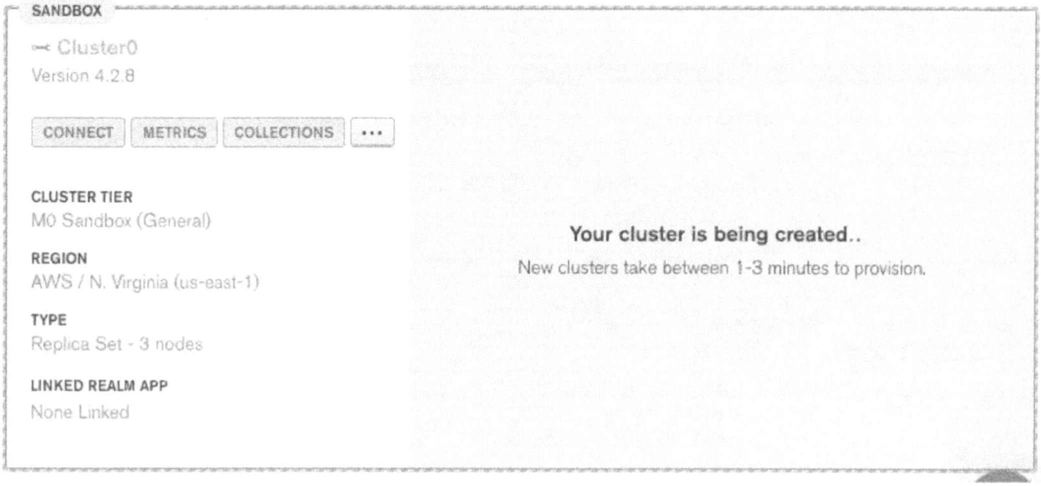

Figure 6

Next, on the left panel, under 'Security', click on 'Database Access' (fig. 7). You should have at least one user who is an admin. You can create a new database admin user by clicking on 'Add New User' and provide him with 'Read and write to any database privileges'.

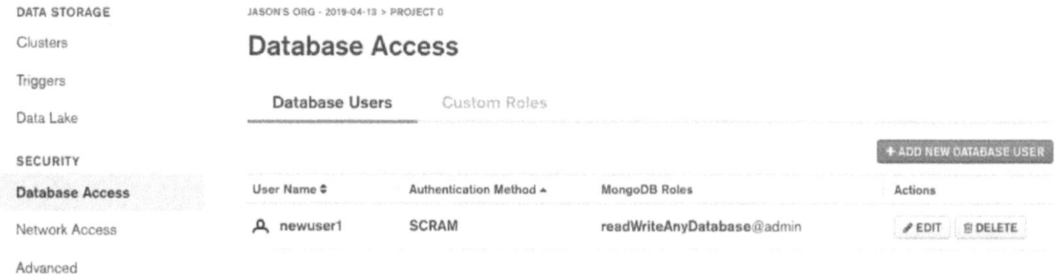

Figure 7

Next, under 'Security', 'Network Access', 'IP Whitelist', add your local IP address. Else, you can't connect to that cluster from your Deno app. Select 'Add IP Address' and enter in your current IP address. Or if you don't know, click on the 'Add Current IP Address' for the site to detect it for you (fig. 8).

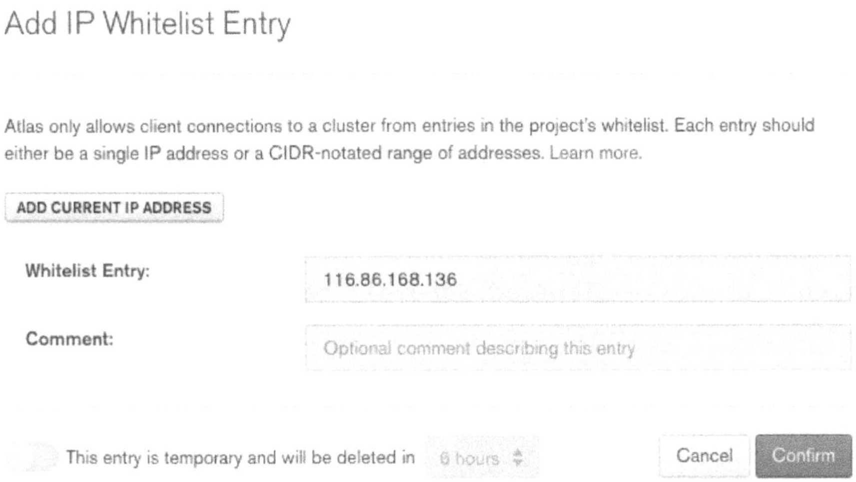

Add IP Whitelist Entry

Atlas only allows client connections to a cluster from entries in the project's whitelist. Each entry should either be a single IP address or a CIDR-notated range of addresses. Learn more.

ADD CURRENT IP ADDRESS

Whitelist Entry: 116.86.168.136

Comment: Optional comment describing this entry

This entry is temporary and will be deleted in   6 hours   Cancel   Confirm

Figure 8

Connecting Deno to MongoDB

Next, let's connect our Deno app to MongoDB. To do so, we use the *deno_mongo* module (https://deno.land/x/mongo). Behind the scenes, Deno is actually written with a language called Rust. And *deno_mongo* is the official Rust MongoDB driver developed by the MongoDB company. The driver exposes functionality that makes it easy to read and write data to the database.

https://deno.land/x/mongo provides an example of how to connect to MongoDB from our app. We will go through it together here.

To connect to the Cloud MongoDB from our app, in our project, we first create a folder 'helper'. 'helper' will store miscellaneous helper files. And in 'helper', create a file named *db.ts*. This file will pertain to database operations. In *db.ts*, fill it with the below code:

```
import { MongoClient, Collection } from
"https://deno.land/x/mongo@v0.9.1/mod.ts";

interface TodoSchema {
  _id: { $oid: string };
```

```
    name: string
}

let todosCollection : Collection<TodoSchema>;

export function connect(){
    const client = new MongoClient();

client.connectWithUri("mongodb+srv://newuser1:uTSXeKFWdmz2wvWa@cluster0.v
xjpr.mongodb.net/?retryWrites=true&w=majority");

    const db = client.database("todos");
    todosCollection = db.collection<TodoSchema>("todos");
}

function getTodosCollection(){
    return todosCollection;
}

export default getTodosCollection;
```

Code Explanation

```
import { MongoClient, Collection } from
"https://deno.land/x/mongo@v0.9.1/mod.ts";
```

MongoClient allows us to connect to the database and interact with it. *Collection* is the type that represents a collection in MongoDB. Remember that data is stored in MongoDB in the form of collections and in each collection, we have documents.

```
interface TodoSchema {
  _id: { $oid: string };
  name: string
}
```

The *TodoSchema* interface represents how a collection looks like. This means that each *document* in the *collection* would have the fields specified in the *TodoSchema*.

You might ask, previously, we already defined our todo object as something like:
{id: "1",name: "Learn Deno1"}. So *name: string* is the same, but why does *id* become _id: { $oid:

`string` } ? This is because currently, we have been generating and assigning our own id. i.e. *id: new Date().toISOString()*. But in MongoDB, every document has a unique id automatically generated by MongoDB and stored in the property *_id*. *_id* in turn stores an object with a string property *$oid* which holds the id.

```
let todosCollection : Collection<TodoSchema>;
```

We then declare `todosCollection` of type *Collection* which points to the collection in our database.

```
export function connect(){
    const client = new MongoClient();

    client.connectWithUri(
       "mongodb+srv://newuser1:uTSXeKFWdmz2wvWa@cluster0.vxjpr.mongodb.net
/?retryWrites=true&w=majority"
    );

    const db = client.database("todos");
    todosCollection = db.collection<TodoSchema>("todos");
}
```

Next, we wrap the database connection related codes in a *connect* method. We do so to make it convenient to call it from *app.ts* as we shall see later (that's why we export it). Also, by putting them in a method, we better ensure that the database connection is made only once and avoid unnecessary multiple database connections.

In `client.connectWithUri`, you have to copy-paste the URL of the MongoDB cluster which you can get from its dashboard. To get the URL, in the MongoDB dashboard main page under 'Clusters', click on 'Connect' (fig. 9):

Figure 9

71

Next, select 'Connect your application' (fig. 10):

Figure 10

And then copy the connection string (fig. 11).

Figure 11

You connection string will look something like:

```
mongodb+srv://newuser1:<password>@cluster0.vxjpr.mongodb.net/<dbname>?ret
ryWrites=true&w=majority
```

You have to fill in your own database username and password. We can remove the database name as we will specify it in code i.e.
```
mongodb+srv://newuser1:<password>@cluster0.vxjpr.mongodb.net/<dbname>?ret
ryWrites=true&w=majority
```

The below line connects the app to our database called 'todos'.

```
const db = client.database("todos");
```

If you have not created the specified database, it will be auto-generated which is really convenient so you don't need to create them in advance. We should mention here that the database connection here is auto-managed by the Mongo module. It auto-manages a connection pool to establish multiple connections. So, if there are multiple simultaneous read/write operations, it will work with all the connection management handled under the hood.

```
todosCollection = db.collection<TodoSchema>("todos");
```

Next, we connect to the 'todos' collection (which again if does not exist in the database, will be auto-created for us). Remember that a *collection* is like an array holding our todo document objects.

```
function getTodosCollection(){
    return todosCollection;
}

export default getTodosCollection;
```

Lastly, we wrap `todosCollection` in a getter method so that when other files require this collection, they can call `getTodosCollection()`. And because we have placed the database connection codes in *connect*, we avoid creating multiple redundant connections.

Connecting from app.ts

Next, we will call connect from *app.ts*. In *app.ts*: add the following in **bold**:

```
import { Application } from "https://deno.land/x/oak/mod.ts";
import router from "./routes/todo-routes.ts";
import { connect } from './helper/db.ts';

connect();
const app = new Application();
...
```

Because *app.ts* is our application's entry point, we open and establish our database connection there. And note that we call *connect()* only once.

Adding a todo

Now, let's try to add a todo to our database. In *todo-routes.ts*, in the *router.post('/add-todo'* handler, make the following changes:

```
import getTodosCollection from '../helper/db.ts';
...
```

```
router.post('/add-todo',async (ctx,next) => {
    const newTodoTitle =  (await ctx.request.body({type:
"form"}).value).get('new-todo');

    if(newTodoTitle && newTodoTitle.trim().length !== 0){
        const newTodo ={id: new Date().toISOString(), name:
newTodoTitle! };
        await getTodosCollection().insertOne(newTodo)
        // we know goalsCollection won't be null

        //todos.push(newTodo);
        console.log(newTodo);
        ctx.response.redirect('/')
    }
    else{
        const todos = await getTodosCollection().find();
        const body = await
renderFileToString(Deno.cwd()+'/views/todos.ejs',{
            title: 'My Todos',
            todos: todos,
            error: "Field cannot be empty"
        });
        ctx.response.body = body;
    }
});
```

Code Explanation

```
import getTodosCollection from '../helper/db.ts';
```

First, import `getTodosCollection`.

```
const newTodo ={id: new Date().toISOString(), name: newTodoTitle! };
```

newTodo now doesn't need the id property because MongoDB will auto-generate it for us.

We then call `await getTodosCollection().insertOne(newTodo)` to insert a todo document into the collection. Because *insertOne* returns a promise, we use the *await* on it to ensure that we complete the insertion before returning to the home page.

```
//todos.push(newTodo);
```

We also remove `todos.push(newTodo)` because we are no longer storing our todos in the application itself.

```
    else{
        const todos = await getTodosCollection().find();
        const body = await
renderFileToString(Deno.cwd()+'/views/todos.ejs',{
            title: 'My Todos',
            todos: todos,
            error: "Field cannot be empty"
        });
        ctx.response.body = body;
    }
```

Lastly, in the *else* clause where we direct the user back to the main page if the field is empty, we retrieve all the todos from the database since now, our todos will not be stored in the array anymore. To retrieve all documents in *todos* collection, we use *getTodosCollection().find()*. If we do not specify anything in *find()*, by default it finds all documents in a collection. We then use await on it because *find* is asynchronous and we wait for it to complete before responding back. We will revisit *find()* in the next section and also later on remove the unused *todos* array from our code.

Running your App

To run your app, we need some extra permissions. Because we are doing a write operation and using the plugin API of Deno which is still in an unstable mode, we need to add the below additional permissions:

```
denon run --allow-net --allow-write --allow-read --allow-plugin --unstable app.ts
```

Now, run your app and add a new todo. After you have done so, go to your MongoDB dashboard and under *Collections*, you should be able to see *todos* collection created for you with the todo document that you have just added (fig. 12).

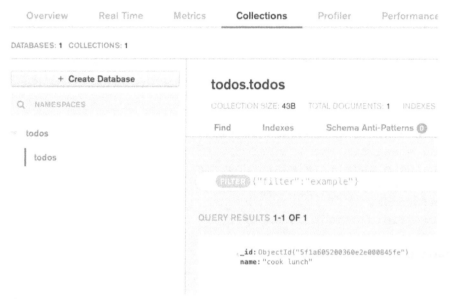

Figure 12

Note the auto-generated *_id* added for you.

You can use this dashboard to visualize your data in the database. Try inserting more todos and see them reflected here.

Reading Data from MongoDB

To retrieve all documents in *todos* collection, in *todo-routes.ts*, add the line into *router.get('/'*...:

```
router.get('/',async (ctx,next)=>{
    const todos = await getTodosCollection().find();
    //console.log("getTodosCollection().find()",todos)
    const body = await renderFileToString(Deno.cwd()+'/views/todos.ejs',{
        title: 'My Todos',
        todos: todos,
        error: null
    });
    ctx.response.body = body;
});
```

Code Explanation

```
await getTodosCollection().find()
```

As mentioned earlier, if we do not specify anything in *find()*, by default it finds all documents in a collection. You can set a filter or restricting the docs you want to retrieve. E.g. to find all todos with a particular name e.g. 'lunch' we do: *await getTodosCollection().find({ name: "lunch" })*. For more on filters for *find*, refer to https://docs.mongodb.com/manual/reference/method/db.collection.find/.

Running your App

When you run your app, you should now see the todos you have stored in MongoDB.
But you will realize that when you click on any of your todo, you are not brought to the view to update them. You will also not be able to delete your todos. And this is because the structure of the object returned from MongoDB is now:

```
{
  _id: { $oid: string },
  name: string
}
```

Where previously, it was:

```
{
  id: string,
  name: string
}
```

From id to _id

To cater to this change, in *todos.ejs*, we have to change *todos[i].id* to *todos[i]._id.$oid*:

```
<% for (let i = 0; i < todos.length;i++){ %>
<a href="/todo/<%= todos[i]._id.$oid %>">
   <li class="list-group-item …">
      <%= todos[i].name %>
      <form action='/delete-todo/<%= todos[i]._id.$oid %>' method="POST">
         <button type="submit" class="btn btn-primary mb-
2">Delete</button>
```

```
    </form>

  </li>
</a>
<% } %>
```

Retrieving a Specific Document from MongoDB

We next have to make changes to *router.get('/todo/:todoId'* so that it retrieves the specific todo from MongoDB.

```
router.get('/todo/:todoId', async (ctx) => {
    const id = ctx.params.todoId!;
    const todo = await getTodosCollection().findOne({ _id: { $oid:
id } });
    //const todo = todos.find(todo => todo.id === id);({ _id: { $oid:
id } })

    if(!todo){
      throw new Error('did not find todo')
  }
    const body = await renderFileToString(Deno.cwd() +
'/views/todo.ejs',{
      todoText: todo.name,
      todoId: todo._id.$oid,
      error: null
    });
    ctx.response.body = body;
}) ;
```

Code Explanation

```
const todo = await getTodosCollection().findOne({ _id: { $oid: id } });
```

The above code is saying in effect, using the *findOne* method, I want to find one document where *_id.$oid* is equal to the id I supplied. Remember that this is because the auto-generated id in MongoDB has this structure:

```
{
  _id: { $oid: string },
  name: string
}
```

The found document is then assigned to *todo* and it's *name* and *id* is passed to *todo.ejs* with:

```
const body = await renderFileToString(Deno.cwd()+'/views/todo.ejs',{
  todoText: todo.name,
  todoId: todo._id.$oid,
  error: null
});
```

Note that we have to add an exclamation to `const id = ctx.params.todoId!` exclamation to fit it into *findOne({ _id: { $oid: id } })*. Specifically, `ctx.params.todoId` returns a type {*string |
undefined*} wherereas we have to specify a strict string in *findOne*. We thus use the '!' to force
`ctx.params.todoId` to return a string.

Running your App

When you run your app now, you should be able to select a todo and be navigated to its update page. But we have yet to implement update for MongoDB. We will go on to do so in the next section.

Updating a Todo in MongoDB

In *router.post('/update-todo/:todoId'*, make the following changes in **bold**:

```
router.post('/update-todo/:todoId', async (ctx) => {
    const id = ctx.params.todoId!;

    const todo = await getTodosCollection().findOne({ _id: { $oid:
id } });
    //const todo = todos.find(todo => todo.id === id);
    if(!todo){
        throw new Error('did not find todo')
    }

    const updatedTodoTitle = (await ctx.request.body({type:
```

```
"form"}).value).get('update-todo');

    if(updatedTodoTitle && updatedTodoTitle.trim().length !== 0){
        todo.name = updatedTodoTitle;
        await getTodosCollection().updateOne(
            {_id: {$oid: id}},
            {$set: {name: updatedTodoTitle}}
        );
        ctx.response.redirect('/')
    }
    else{
        const body = await
renderFileToString(Deno.cwd()+'/views/todo.ejs',{
            todoText: todo.name,
            todoId: todo._id.$oid,
            error: "Field cannot be empty"
        });
        ctx.response.body = body;
    }
});
```

Code Explanation

```
const id = ctx.params.todoId!;
```

Just like in retrieving a specific todo, we add an exclamation to **const id =
ctx.params.todoId!** exclamation to later fit it into *updateOne({ _id: { $oid: id } }).*

```
    const todo = await getTodosCollection().findOne({ _id: { $oid:
id } });
    //const todo = todos.find(todo => todo.id === id);
```

We retrieve the todo to be updated using *findOne* as we are no longer using the *todos* array.

```
await getTodosCollection().updateOne(
    {_id: {$oid: id}},
    {$set: {name: updatedTodoTitle}}
);
```

We then update the todo with *updateOne*. *$set* is a special property name recognized by MongoDB to

80

define which object should be set or which fields be set to new values, in our case `{name: updatedTodoTitle}`. And again, because *updateOne* is asynchronous and returns a Promise, we use *await* on it to ensure that the update operation is completed before we redirect back to the user.

```
    else{
        const body = await
renderFileToString(Deno.cwd()+'/views/todo.ejs',{
            todoText: todo.name,
            todoId: todo._id.$oid,
            error: "Field cannot be empty"
        });
        ctx.response.body = body;
    }
```

And if `updatedTodoTitle` is empty, we direct the user back to the update page with a warning, and *todoId: todo._id.$oid*.

Running your App

When we run our app now, we should able to update a todo. Let's finally move on to delete.

Deleting a Todo in MongoDB

Finally for deleting a todo, in *router.post('/delete-todo/:todoId'*, add the below line:

```
router.post('/delete-todo/:todoId', async (ctx) => {
    const id = ctx.params.todoId!;
  await getTodosCollection().deleteOne({_id:{$oid: id}});
    //todos = todos.filter(todo => todo.id !== id);
    ctx.response.redirect('/');
});
```

deleteOne targets the specific document in a fashion similar to *findOne* and *updateOne*.
Again, we place the *await* statement to ensure that deletion completes first before we redirect back to the main page.

Running your App

When you run your app, you will be able to delete todos. And these are our C.R.U.D. operations implemented with MongoDB.

And because we are storing and retrieving todos from MongoDB, we should get rid of *todos* array in *todos-route.ts*. So, remove the following from *todos-route.ts*:

```
let todos: {id: String, name: String }[] = {
    {id: "1",name: "Learn Deno1"},
    {id: "2",name: "Prepare lunch"},
    {id: "3",name: "Read bible"}
};
```

Introducing the MVC Pattern

In the course of building the app, let's take a moment to zoom out and understand our code's organization. I have actually applied the MVC architecture pattern to our simple project.

If you are not familiar with MVC, MVC stands for Model View Controller. It is a way of organizing your files and code to separate it in a logical standardized way to make it easy for you and other developers to understand and work with your code. This is to ensure that code is maintainable when our app grows.

- *Model* represents the structure of the data, the format and the constraints with which it is stored. In essence, it is the database part of the application. We have that in */helper/db.ts* file which defines the *Todo* Schema and connection to the database.

- *View* is what is presented to the user. Views make use of the Model and present data in a manner which the user wants. From the view, user can make changes to the data presented to them. In our app, the View consist of static or dynamic pages rendered to users. In our *views* folder, we have various EJS files to render static and dynamic HTML to show a list of todos and forms to add, update todos.

- Lastly, we have *Controller* which controls the requests of the user and then generates appropriate responses to them. That is, a user interacts with the View to generate a request which is handled by the Controller and renders the appropriate view with the Model data as a response. For example, we have *todo-routes.ts* which work with *db.ts* to provide C.R.U.D. operations to the todos and then handling that data off to the views thereafter.

In structuring our project code into the Model-View-Controller pattern, we make our code more manageable and organised.

Summary

We were introduced to MongoDB, a NoSQL database that stores data in the form of collections and documents. Using *deno_mongo*, we connected our Deno application with the Mongo database. We defined the *ToDoSchema* interface to represent the collections in our database. We illustrated Create, Read, Update and Delete operations via *deno_mongo*. Finally, we saw how our app fit into the MVC architecture.

Refer to https://github.com/greglim81/deno_chapter7 for the source code of this chapter. If you face any issues, contact me at support@i-ducate.com.

CHAPTER 8: BUILDING REST APIS WITH DENO

So far, we have built a web app that serves server-side rendered views through templates. We can also just build APIs to serve data to clients like mobile apps and browsers who then render the retrieved data on their front-end UI. In this chapter, we look at how we build REST APIs with Deno.

We will build a product API to facilitate C.R.U.D. of products. For e.g.:

```
{
  id: "1",
  name: "Product One",
  description: "This is product one",
  price: 99.99,
},
{
  id: "2",
  name: "Product Two",
  description: "This is product two",
  price: 150.99,
},
{
  id: "3",
  name: "Product Three",
  description: "This is product three",
  price: 199.99,
}
```

The API will have a couple of endpoints. Suppose we have *mydomain.com*:
- To fetch a list of products, send a GET request to *mydomain.com/products*
- To add a product, send a POST request to *mydomain.com/products*
- To update a product, send a PATCH request to *mydomain.com/products/:productid*
- To delete a product, send a DELETE request to *mydomain.com/products/:productId*

To quickstart building our project, we will duplicate the folder from our project in the last chapter and then make changes to it. This is because many of the folder structure and files are similar. That way, we do not have to repeat building files like *app.ts*, or re-create folders like *routes*, *helper*. However, we no longer need the *views* folder as we are not rendering any views. So, we can delete it.

/helper/db.ts

In the newly copied project, in */helper/db.ts*, rename *todos* to *products* and also add fields to *ProductSchema* as shown below in **bold**:

```
import { MongoClient, Collection } from
"https://deno.land/x/mongo@v0.9.1/mod.ts";

interface ProductSchema {
  _id: { $oid: string };
  name: string;
  description: string;
  price: number;
}

let productsCollection : Collection<ProductSchema>;

export function connect(){
    const client = new MongoClient();

client.connectWithUri("mongodb+srv://newuser1:uTSXeKFWdmz2wvWa@cluster0.v
xjpr.mongodb.net/?retryWrites=true&w=majority");

    const db = client.database("products");

    productsCollection = db.collection<ProductSchema>("products");
}

function getProductsCollection(){
    return productsCollection;
}

export default getProductsCollection;
```

Endpoint to Add a Product

Next, in the *routes* folder, we will delete *todo-routes.ts* and instead create a new file *product-routes.ts*. We will first implement the endpoint to add a product i.e. a POST request to */products*.
Fill *product-routes.ts* with the below codes:

```
import { Router } from "https://deno.land/x/oak/mod.ts";
import getProductsCollection from '../helper/db.ts';

const router = new Router();

router.post('/products',async (ctx,next) => {
    const data = await ctx.request.body({type: "json"}).value;
    const name = data.name;
    const description = data.description;
    const price = data.price;

    /* you can validate values here e.g. if its empty
    if(...)
    */

    const id = await getProductsCollection()!.insertOne({
        name: name,
        description: description,
        price: price
    });
    ctx.response.body = {id: id.$oid};
});

export default router;
```

Code Explanation

```
import { Router } from "https://deno.land/x/oak/mod.ts";
import getProductsCollection from '../helper/db.ts';

const router = new Router();
```

Like what we did in *todo-routes.ts*, we import *Router* and *getProductsCollection*, our database helper. Note that we no longer have to import *renderFileToString* because we are not rendering EJS files anymore.

```
router.post('/products',async (ctx,next) => {
```

We implement the route handler for a POST request to */products* to add a product.

```
const data = await ctx.request.body({type: "json"}).value;
```

We expect that the request body comes in a json format (we will demonstrate sending a POST request with json to this route later). Thus, we specify type: "json". Because *value* is a Promise which returns the json object, we thus use *await*.

```
const name = data.name;
const description = data.description;
const price = data.price;
```

We next extract the name, description and price from the json object.

```
const id = await getProductsCollection()!.insertOne({
    name: name,
    description: description,
    price: price
});
```

We then insert the extracted values into our MongoDB with *insertOne* similar to what we have done in our todos app.

```
ctx.response.body = {id: id.$oid};
```

We then respond with the object `{id: id.$oid}` . Remember that MongoDB auto-generates an id for us in the structure *_id.$oid*. To simplify the response and give id directly to the user, we have `{id: id.$oid}` e.g.:

```
{
    "id": "5f1d30ca0047230400813ae0"
}
```

Note that the Oak module auto-translates the response body to json. Whenever you set a body that's an object, it will be sent back as a json.

app.ts

Now, in *app.ts*, we just need to make one change:

```
import router from "./routes/product-routes.ts";
```

Running and Testing your App

Run your app by executing:

```
denon run --allow-net --allow-write --allow-read --allow-plugin --unstable app.ts
```

Previously, we could just visit the web page in the browser and add a todo to test if our route works. But this is not possible for testing with APIs. However, we can use a special tool called Postman (https://www.postman.com/). Download it for free on its site and install it.

In Postman, you can open tabs to send GET, POST and other kinds of requests (fig. 1).

Figure 1

In a new tab, select a POST request to *localhost:8000/products* where our Deno server is running. Now, how do we send the values along with the request to add a product? You can provide the values under 'Body'. Then go to 'raw', and select 'JSON' in the dropdown. Then, add your json in curly braces (fig. 2).

Figure 2

Click send and we should get back the id of the newly added product as response (fig. 3):

Figure 3

This is because we have earlier defined the response as:

```
ctx.response.body = {id: id.$oid};
```

Endpoint to Getting Products

Next, let's implement the get products endpoint. In *product-routes.ts*, add the following:

```
router.get('/products', async (ctx,next) => {

    const products = await getProductsCollection()!.find();

    const productsFormatted = products.map((product: any) => ({
      id: product._id.$oid,
      name: product.name,
      description: product.description,
```

```
    price: product.price
  }));

  ctx.response.body = {products: productsFormatted};
});
```

Code Explanation

```
router.get('/products'
```

The above route handler handles GET requests to */products*. Note that it shares the same URL *'/products'* as our earlier POST request, and later on, our PATCH and DELETE requests. But because we are using different HTTP methods, only one route will kick in at a time.

```
const products = await getProductsCollection()!.find();
```

We extract the products from MongoDB. We can return *products* as our response. But if we do so, the structure returned is something like:

```
{
    "products": [
        {
            "_id": {
                "$oid": "5f1d30ca0047230400813ae0"
            },
            "name": "Product 1",
            "description": "Desc 1",
            "price": 1.99
        }
    ]
}
```

which complicates the retrieval of *id*. It is better that we simplify this structure to:

```
{
    "products": [
        {
            "id": "5f1d30ca0047230400813ae0",
            "name": "Product 1",
            "description": "Desc 1",
            "price": 1.99
        }
    ]
}
```

91

To do so, we call the *map* function of products:

```
const productsFormatted = products.map((product: any) => ({
  id: product._id.$oid,
  name: product.name,
  description: product.description,
  price: product.price
}));
```

With *map*, we go through each product and return a new object where we assign **product._id.$oid** to *id*, and copy the rest of the properties. This makes it convenient for the client so they can access the *id* field in the response directly.

Running and Testing our App

Back in Postman, change the request to 'GET' with URL localhost:8000/products and hit 'Send' (fig. 4).

Figure 4

And you will get a response like:
```
{
    "products": [
        {
            "id": "5f1d30ca0047230400813ae0",
            "name": "Product 1",
            "description": "Desc 1",
            "price": 1.99
        }
    ]
}
```

With this, we have implemented our API endpoints for creating and retrieving products. Try adding more products and retrieving them on your own. And you will get *products* like:

```json
{
    "products": [
        {
            "id": "5f1d30ca0047230400813ae0",
            "name": "Product 1",
            "description": "Desc 1",
            "price": 1.99
        },
        {
            "id": "5f1e3fb600a1d34900197da8",
            "name": "Product 2",
            "description": "Desc 2",
            "price": 10.99
        }
        ...
    ]
}
```

Endpoint to Update a Product

To provide an endpoint to update a product, add the below router handler for
router.patch('/products/:productId':

```javascript
router.patch('/products/:productId', async (ctx) => {
    const data = await ctx.request.body({type: "json"}).value;
    const id = ctx.params.productId!;

    const updatedProduct = await getProductsCollection()!.updateOne(
      {_id: {$oid: id}},{$set: data}
    );

    ctx.response.body = {
        updatedProduct: updatedProduct
    };
});
```

93

Code Explanation

```
router.patch('/products/:productId'
```

The update API endpoint expects a PATCH request with an object sent to the route */products/:productid*.

```
const data = await ctx.request.body({type: "json"}).value;
const id = ctx.params.productId!;
```

Similar to the POST request, we extract the data from the incoming request. We also extract the id of the document to be updated from the id placeholder. Note that we place an exclamation to explicitly specify that id can't be null.

```
const updatedProduct = await getProductsCollection()!.updateOne(
  {_id: {$oid: id}},{$set: data}
);
```

In *updateOne*, we specify *id* in the first argument *{_id: {$oid: id}}* to specify which document to update. We then set *data* as the second argument to update all fields with the values in *data*. Remember that *$set* is a special property name recognized by MongoDB to define which object should be set or which fields be set to new values.

```
ctx.response.body = {
    updatedProduct: updatedProduct
};
```

We then respond with the results of the update.

Running our App

Go to Postman, open a new tab and specify a PATCH request. Provide the URL and a product id to update (fig. 5).

Figure 5

And like in adding a product, select 'Body', 'raw', 'JSON' and specify the update values in json. Hit

'Send' and we should get a result (fig. 6):

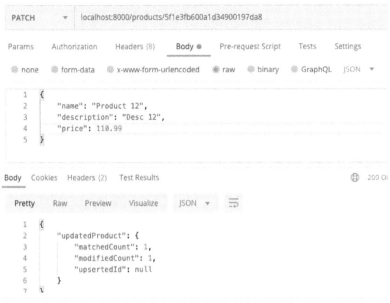

Figure 6

Endpoint to Delete a Product

To have an endpoint to delete a product, add the below router handler into *product-routes.ts*:

```
router.delete('/products/:productId', async (ctx) => {
    const id = ctx.params.productId!;
    await getProductsCollection()!.deleteOne({_id:{$oid: id}});
    ctx.response.body = {
        message: "deleted " + id
    };
});
```

The delete code by now should be quite familiar to you. So let's go ahead to run and test this.

In Postman, create a new tab and change the request type to 'DELETE'. Enter a URL with the product id to be deleted and hit 'Send'.

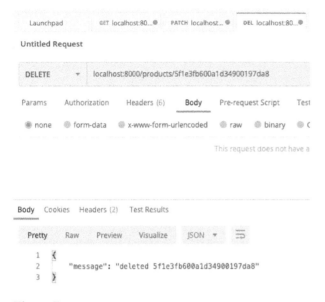

Figure 7

You should receive a response like in (fig. 7).

Cross-Origin Resource Sharing (CORS)

We want frontend clients to talk to our REST API to fetch or send data. But by default, modern browsers don't allow this interaction. They block requests sent from clients to the server as a security mechanism to make sure that client-side browser JavaScript code can only talk to their own allowed server and not to some other servers which can potentially run malicious code.

Now, when we build an API, we do want to expose it to all kinds of server, else no one is able to use our API. To circumvent this security mechanism, we can enable CORS checking. Cross-Origin Resource Sharing (CORS) is a mechanism that uses additional HTTP headers to tell browsers to give a web application running at one origin, access to selected resources from a different origin.

On the server, we can set specific response headers to the responses we send back to the client to let the browser know that we are fine with returning that information. And that the browser should not block it. We can configure our server to allow this access. In Postman, we didn't have any problems because Postman doesn't have this security concept.

So, on the server, in *app.ts*, we set headers that grant client access to our resources. We do this with a

Deno third-party library (https://deno.land/x/cors@v1.1.0#cors) that provides a middleware that can be used to enable CORS with various options.

In *app.ts*, add the lines in **bold**:

```
import { Application } from "https://deno.land/x/oak/mod.ts";
import router from "./routes/product-routes.ts";
import { connect } from './helper/db.ts';
import { oakCors } from "https://deno.land/x/cors/mod.ts";

connect();

const app = new Application();

app.use(oakCors()); // Enable CORS for All Routes
...
...
...
```

Code Explanation

We import the CORS module and call *app.use(oakCors())* to enable CORS for all routes.

To provide further options, we can provide an *options* object. For e.g.

```
app.use(
  oakCors({
    origin: "*",
    methods: "GET,PATCH,POST,DELETE"
  }),
);
```

In *origin*, we can set which domains are allowed to access this API. '*' grants any server access to this API. We can also restrict it to 'some-domain.com'. For example, if you set it to "http://example.com" only requests from "http://example.com" will be allowed.

In *methods*, you configure which HTTP request methods are allowed to be sent. Here, we allow GET, POST, PATCH and DELETE which are the request we use in our routes. For e.g. we are not using PUT.

Summary

We have implemented our REST APIs to support C.R.U.D. of products which we can expose to clients. The simulated client that we have used here is Postman, but in a real-world app, it would typically be a mobile app or web app.

Implementing a client-side mobile app or web app to consume REST APIs is obviously beyond this book's scope. But I have written a book on developing web frontends with React to consume REST APIs. And if you are interested in getting a copy, contact me at support@i-ducate.com.

Refer to https://github.com/greglim81/deno_chapter8 for the source code of this chapter. If you face any issues, contact me at support@i-ducate.com.

CHAPTER 9: COMPARING DENO AND NODE

Having implemented a web app and a REST API with Deno, we are now more familiar with it. It is then time to recap and dwell into a more meaningful comparison of Deno and Node.

TypeScript Support

An advantage Deno has over Node is that it has built-in TypeScript support. We can certainly use TypeScript in Node but that involves manual installations of 3rd party compilers whereas in Deno, we just use TypeScript out of the box and not worry about any additional configurations.

To provide an example of an advantage using TypeScript, it allows the typing feature. When we define variables, we can specify their type. For example:

```
let name: string;
let description: string;
let price: number;
```

Whereas JavaScript by default doesn't support types:

```
let name;
let description;
let price;
```

Because TypeScript enforces type checking, it helps us to identify issues earlier. In general, we try to avoid 'any' as much as possible.

Promises

Next, Deno being based on modern JavaScript features means it embraces Promises. Node being a bit older is based on older JavaScript code which doesn't really support Promises (except only for newer Node versions). Instead, Node typically uses callback functions for asynchronous code.

When an asynchronous function finishes, a promise is informed. And with modern JavaScript, we can use *async/await* (and top-level *await* without *async*) to make it so that asynchronous code looks like synchronous code which to shorter, more concise and readable code. It avoids the dreaded 'callback hell'. Technically, Node works fine using callbacks but is just not as elegant as modern JavaScript code.

Imports

We have seen that Deno supports URL imports where we point to other files. It is actually inspired by the *Go* programming language where it doesn't leave room for confusion as to what we are importing and where we are importing it from. It is neither necessary to keep a list of dependencies in a *package.json* file nor have all modules visible in *node_modules* like in Node.

Node on the other hand uses *require* and *module.export* syntax e.g. *const express = require('express')* and this leads to another difference. That is, how the imported libraries are stored which we discuss in the next section.

Libraries

In Node, third party libraries need to be installed locally. To *require* a file on a third-party library, we have to use *npm install* to download and install the library into the *node_modules* folder along with their dependencies. The installations are then managed through the *package.json* file. The *node_modules* folder can take considerable space in the hard drive.

With Deno, the difference is that we directly import files from the third party. Deno will still download the file and cache it locally so that you won't need to download it each time you run the script. But this saves you the extra step of installing everything before you launch your app. There is also no unwieldy *package.json* file nor massive *node_modules* folder.

Security

Another difference is when we execute Deno scripts, we have to specify permissions. In the course of this book, we ran applications which accessed the internet and required us to specify *--allow-net*. When our app had to read a file i.e. *renderFileToString*, we had to specify *--allow-read*.

In this way, it prevents the scenario of someone running a malicious script that can potentially delete all of your files on your computer which is possible in Node as Node doesn't require such execution permissions. But in Deno, unless you explicitly give your program the ability to delete files from your computer, that script will not be able to do anything because it doesn't have the permission. So Deno in terms of security offers an advantage in having these permissions built in.

So, do we just abandon Node and focus on Deno?

With the additional features mentioned, it looks like Deno is better. So, will Deno just replace Node and we all focus on Deno and forget about Node? Now, Deno is still new and there will naturally be bugs. There is also no big ecosystem yet. Node however has been around for a much longer time, is an established and mature system used by many major companies. It has no major bugs, is supported by a huge team and has a strong ecosystem.

Also, not being able to use *npm* with Deno is actually a bit of a downside because there are so many *npm* packages out there. Many of them are not compatible with Deno out of the box e.g. 3rd party libraries to deal with sessions, authentications etc. So, Deno is in a sense missing out on a huge portion of what makes Node so popular. And it will be a while before the community writes more Deno-based packages.

Deno and Node actually share many similarities

Before you start to feel discouraged thinking that you have wasted all these time learning Deno, let me tell you that Deno and Node share many more similarities than differences. Many concepts like middlewares, routes, handling requests and responses are brought over from Node into Deno and work in the same way.

Most importantly, the code from one isn't too far from the other. For example, in Deno we might have:

```
import { Application, Router } from "https://deno.land/x/oak/mod.ts";

const app = new Application();
const router = new Router();

router.get('/',(ctx,next)=>{
    ctx.response.body = `<h1>The home page\n</h1>`
    ctx.response.type = 'text/html';
});

router.get('/contact',(ctx,next)=>{
    ctx.response.body = `<h1>The contact page\n</h1>`
    ctx.response.type = 'text/html';
});
```

```
app.use(router.routes());
app.use(router.allowedMethods());

await app.listen({ port: 8000 });
```

In Node, the code would look something like:

```
const express = require('express');

const app = express();
const router = express.Router();

router.get('/',(req,res)=>{
    res.send('<h1>The home page\n</h1>');
});

router.get('/contact',(ctx,next)=>{
    res.send('<h1>The contact page\n</h1>');
});

app.use(router);
app.listen(8000);
```

See the similarities? Knowing one will put you in a good position to know the other. In fact, I have written a best selling Node development book. You can contact me at support@i-ducate.com to get a copy.

Where do we go from here?

Because Deno is still under active development, it will be useful to periodically refer to its official page (https://deno.land/ - fig. 1) to keep up with changes. Explore the 'Runtime API' to learn more about core features in Deno for example, working with files, sending HTTP requests.

| | Install | Manual | Runtime API | Standard Library | Third Party Modules | |

Deno

A **secure** runtime for **JavaScript** and **TypeScript**.

Figure 1

Explore the 'Standard Library' and 'Third-Party Modules'. Many modules help with all kinds of things and are worth checking out.

Also check out Deno's official GitHub page (https://github.com/denoland) where development on Deno happens.

With that, you have a thorough introduction to Deno and have all the tools you need to explore it on your own and build your own side projects.

Final Words

We have gone through quite a lot of content to equip you with the skills to create a Deno app with Oak and MongoDB.

Hopefully, you have enjoyed this book and would like to learn more from me. I would love to get your feedback, learning what you liked and didn't for us to improve.

Please feel free to email me at support@i-ducate.com if you encounter any errors with your code or to get updated versions of this book.

If you didn't like the book, or feel that I should have covered certain additional topics, please email us to let us know. This book can only get better thanks to readers like you.

If you like the book, I would appreciate if you could leave us a review too. Thank you and all the best for your learning journey in Deno development!

ABOUT THE AUTHOR

Greg Lim is a technologist and author of several programming books. Greg has many years in teaching programming in tertiary institutions and he places special emphasis on learning by doing.

Contact Greg at support@i-ducate.com.

Lightning Source UK Ltd.
Milton Keynes UK
UKHW030951250920
370514UK00008B/1024